MW01296718

A Pioneering and Independent Spirit:

The History of San José State University's School of Library and Information Science

---

By

Debra Gold Hansen

Order this book online at www.trafford.com

or email orders@trafford.com

Most Trafford titles are also available at major online book retailers.

Printed in Victoria, BC, Canada.

ISBN: 978-1-4269-2109-4 (soft)
ISBN: 978-1-4269-2108-7 (hard)

Library of Congress Control Number: 2009912056

Our mission is to efficiently provide the world's finest, most comprehensive book publishing service, enabling every author to experience success. To find out how to publish your book, your way, and have it available worldwide, visit us online at www.trafford.com

Trafford rev. 3/17/2010

www.trafford.com

North America & international
toll-free: 1 888 232 4444 (USA & Canada)
phone: 250 383 6864 • fax: 812 355 4082

San José State University
School of Library and Information Science

San José, California

Contents

Introduction

In June 2007, the American Library Association's Committee on Accreditation (COA) awarded San José State University's School of Library and Information Science (SLIS) a full seven-year accreditation, the maximum period possible. In its evaluation, COA's review panel extolled SLIS's energy and entrepreneurial spirit in developing and delivering a highly successful academic and professional program. "The combination of affordability, visionary leadership, and accessible technology," the team concluded, "has resulted in the school emerging as (to quote the director) 'the world's largest accredited [LIS] graduate program'" (Annual Report, 2005-2007, p. 5, SLIS Archives).

Since reaccreditation in 2007, SLIS continues to grow and prosper. It now supports four separate degree programs: Master of Library and Information Science (MLIS), Executive MLIS, Teacher Librarian Services Credential, and Master of Archives and Records Administration (MARA). In August 2008, SLIS inaugurated an international Gateway PhD program in partnership with Australia's Queensland University of Technology. Teaching more than 50 courses a semester, SLIS offers a variety of specializations, ranging from reference and information services to information architecture, systems, and design. Currently, the school employs 18 full-time and over 150 part-time instructors; their combined experience and expertise infuse the curriculum with unrivaled depth and breadth. In the spring of 2009, SLIS's student body topped 2,800, with applications for future semesters at an all-time high. These students were not only coming from nearby locales, but were drawn from all over the country, indeed from all over the world. SLIS's cutting-edge technology and incomparable technical support staff has enabled this army of instructors and students to forge a virtual educational community in which significant professional learning and socialization take place.

What accounts for SLIS's phenomenal growth and success? The following historical account seeks to illuminate SLIS's evolution from 1928 to 2009, as it grew from a small school library training program into a comprehensive graduate school of library and information science. Chapter 1 provides a background and context for SLIS's story by describing the university's history and California's changing educational environment that created an interest in and need for a library training program in San José. Chapter 2 introduces the key figures who established the Department of Librarianship in 1928 and discusses the issues they faced in developing the program's original mission and goals. Chapter 3 considers the program's important role in educating teacher-librarians for the state's public schools and reviews the challenges wrought by the Great Depression and World War II. The next chapter explores the Department of Librarianship's postwar expansion and the impact in the 1950s and 1960s that new information technologies would have on library science training. This chapter also charts SLIS's successful bid in 1969 to earn American Library Association (ALA) accreditation. Accreditation issues dominate Chapter 5, as SLIS (and SJSU) faced in the early 1970s a nearly catastrophic economic crisis that resulted in a temporary loss of ALA accreditation. This chapter recounts SLIS's subsequent reaccreditation and assesses the impact of the computer revolution on SLIS curriculum, faculty, and students. Chapter 6 focuses on the development in the 1990s of SLIS's distance education program and the school's experimentation with emerging technologies to widen its reach. Starting with a discussion of SLIS's branch campus in Southern California, this final chapter recounts why San José State's School of Library and Information Science developed its off-campus program and how it ultimately became the largest MLIS program in the world.

It is a propitious time to be writing this history, for in March 2009 SLIS took another bold step by going completely online. This means that now SLIS is not only the world's largest MLIS program, it is also the first wholly virtual one. In this time of rapid change and expansion, it is easy to forget the program's past and the many forward-looking people who contributed to its history. As with current administrators, faculty, and students, these earlier individuals were pioneers who developed new paths to professional education. They confronted many challenges along the way and persevered in adverse times. This history is a tribute to these unsung individuals who helped make SLIS the success it is today.

Acknowledgments

It is with heartfelt gratitude that I acknowledge the many individuals who assisted in the research and writing of *A Pioneering and Independent Spirit.* Although I am responsible for this history's presentation and interpretation, the compilation of SLIS's historical data has truly been a team effort. SLIS students Brian Chambers, Livia Hirsch-Shell, Elizabeth Newsom, Christine Doan, and Traci Bergerson comprised the original research team. During the 2006 summer session, they conducted a thoroughgoing records survey and compiled the first comprehensive, multi-repository inventory of SLIS records. In 2007 and 2008, other student-colleagues devoted countless hours to collecting and synthesizing data, and each of the book's chapters reflect the scholarship done by these individuals: Traci Bergerson and Carla Garner, who researched SLIS faculty; Judy Strebel, Kathleen Brantley-Gutierrez, and Amy Goldsmith, who studied SLIS students; Michael Murray, who examined SLIS's distance education program; and Antoinette Avila, who created a list of SLIS lecturers and speakers.

The voluminous data included in this study was obtained due to the professional assistance and cooperation of librarians and archivists at the American Library Association Archives, the Bancroft Library, the California State Library, and the University Archives and Special Collections Section at California State University, Fullerton's Pollak Library. A particular debt is owed to Danelle Moon and her assistants at SJSU's Dr. Martin Luther King, Jr. Library Special Collections and Archives, who were extremely helpful in locating SLIS records and assisting SLIS research assistants in their work. I also thank SLIS Associate Director Linda Main, office managers Brenda Lamb and Gina Lee, and other SLIS staff for providing information buried in the school's records. The editorial work performed by Susan Sang and Arthur Hansen was invaluable and deeply appreciated.

Finally, I gratefully acknowledge SLIS Director Ken Haycock for the important role he played in the making of this publication. Not only did he have the original inspiration that the School of Library and Information Science deserved a full historical treatment, but it was through his continued financial support and personal encouragement that the current study was completed.

Chapter 1

The Origins of a University and Its Library School

> Sealed in the vaults of memory, the year 1928-29, one of unprecedented expansion scholastically, athletically, structurally, will live forever. The future greatness of our *alma mater* needs no tribute—such we feel, is insured.
>
> *La Torre*
> 1929

San José State taught its first library science courses in the fall of 1928. It was an academic year of singular importance, as the college community encountered new buildings, new academic programs, and a new administration. San José State's 1,500 students could select from several academic programs and earn a bachelor's or associate of arts degree or the traditional teaching credential. President Thomas MacQuarrie had embarked upon an ambitious plan to develop the college into a major economic, social, and cultural force in the region. Although these changes in Washington Square appeared sudden and dramatic, in actuality they represented the culmination of a statewide, progressive educational movement that began many years earlier. This chapter will review the origins and evolution of San José State

University within this wider context to shed light on why it established a Department of Librarianship in 1928.

Founding of San José State Teacher's College

San José State enjoys the distinction of being California's first publicly funded institution of higher education. Its progenitor was Minns Evening Normal School, founded by the City of San Francisco in 1857 to provide pedagogical training to current and aspiring teachers. Minns School operated for five years and graduated 54 students, all women.

In 1862 the California State Legislature passed Senate Bill No. 408, which officially established the "California State Normal School" under the aegis of the State Board of Education. Located in San Francisco, the State Normal School supplanted Minns School as the official public agency responsible for teacher training in California. In 1863, James Swett, a former Minns faculty,[1] was elected State Superintendent of Public Schools. With first-hand knowledge of teachers and teaching conditions, Swett instituted major changes in the state's educational system, including teacher certification and the establishment of school libraries, at least at the district level.

By the late 1860s, Normal School administrators and state officials were growing dissatisfied with the condition and location of its Market Street facility. The State Board of Education considered relocating the Normal School to a different location within San Francisco or merging it with the newly created university at Berkeley. Current Superintendent of Public Schools, Oscar Fitzgerald, rejected both options. He feared that at Berkeley the Normal School would be marginalized, reduced to "a sickly little plant in the shade of a great oak" (as quoted in Gilbert, 1957, p. 47). A Methodist minister, Fitzgerald also disliked putting a school whose faculty and students were predominantly women in an urbanized, commercial center like San Francisco. In Fitzgerald's view, under current conditions the Normal School was like "a drop of literature" in "an ocean of mammon" (as quoted in Gilbert, p. 47).

[1] Swett was married to Mary Lindsay, who taught at the State Normal School from1862 to1867. She served as the Normal School's vice-principal from 1865 to1867.

Thomas Lucky, who served as the Normal School's principal from 1868 to 1873, concurred with Fitzgerald's judgment. Also an ordained Methodist minister who taught courses in the "moral and intellectual sciences," Lucky believed that female students must be properly supervised. The availability of a boardinghouse suitable for young women was among his top priorities in selecting a new school site.

Several cities competed for the opportunity to have the California State Normal School relocated to their community. Stockton, Napa, Vallejo, and Martinez all lobbied the state legislature to select their town for the new campus. San José promoters lauded their city's central location, modern transportation system, and superior climate in their bid to become the school's new home. Although in 1870 San José was the third largest city in California, with a population of only 9,000, it lacked many of the urban problems that plagued San Francisco and Sacramento. Despite its modest size, San José enjoyed a thriving economy and many cultural amenities, including an opera house, lyceum, music hall, and public gardens. A literate community, San Joséans also supported five local newspapers, a good bookstore, and a social library.[2] To make their offer to the state even more attractive, San José promised to donate a 27-acre park known as "Washington Square" for the new campus buildings.

Superintendent Fitzgerald and Principal Lucky were won over by San José's advantages, and they pressured the state legislature to move the Normal School to the Santa Clara Valley. As Fitzgerald explained,

> All things considered, San Jose is, in my judgment, the proper location for the State Normal School. It meets every requirement. The climate is unsurpassed, the place is large enough to furnish all needed facilities for boarding, the training school, etc.; it is accessible from all parts of the state; the people are intelligent, hospitable, and moral. . . . At San Jose the Normal School would be an object of local pride and attachment, while, like "a city set on a hill," it would cast its beams of light over the whole state. (As quoted in Gilbert, p. 47)

[2] A social library was a library and reading room funded by individual donations.

The legislature acquiesced, and the California State Normal School opened in San José in June of 1871. In 1887, the school's name was changed to San José State Normal School, to differentiate it from other normal schools established elsewhere in the state.

Until 1920, California's normal schools specialized exclusively in teacher training, awarding students a teaching credential upon completion of the required coursework. However, in the 1920s major changes in California's educational system prompted normal schools to enlarge their original mission and scope. In 1921, the California State Legislature created the Department of Education (under the governance of California's Board of Education and Superintendent of Public Schools), and this new agency modernized the state's educational infrastructure and instituted a series of progressive reforms. The department assumed direction of the normal schools and turned them into four-year undergraduate colleges. It also codified and standardized existing public schooling laws, producing California's first comprehensive Education Code in 1928. This new state education code raised the minimum qualifications for teacher certification and increased the years of schooling required to become a classroom teacher.

The Department of Education also developed a number of special credentials to enforce higher standards for teaching required subjects. Among these was a "Special Credential in Librarianship," adopted in 1928. Now, according to California state law, any individual working in a school library for more than two hours a day must possess a teaching credential and have completed 24 units of professional coursework from an American Library Association-accredited library school.[3]

San José State Normal School thus became San José State Teacher's College in 1921. As a college, San José State could offer a four-year bachelor of arts degree in education in addition to the teaching credential. In 1923 San José State added a junior college program for students seeking an associate of arts degree or desiring to earn units that would transfer to the University of California. By 1928, San José State had become a comprehensive, degree-granting institution supporting a number of teaching and non-teaching undergraduate specializations.

[3] California was one of only 21 states that required a special certificate for school librarians at that time.

San José State Teachers College, 1928-1929

A key player in San José State's transformation from a normal school to a state college was Thomas W. MacQuarrie, an education "modernist" appointed college president in 1927. MacQuarrie ruled the college with an iron hand and exercised absolute authority over all campus matters (Walsh, 2003, p. 2). He valued practical, applied educational programs, and his ambition was to prepare San José State students for a variety of occupations in support of the region's burgeoning economy. As the president explained in his 1929 State of the School message:

> [W]e have developed out of the field of a limited teacher-training institution, and we are rapidly taking on the character of the modern, municipal college. We are now in a position to select and train teachers better than ever before, and we are also able to train those who should not become teachers, or do not wish to follow that profession. Our organization, as it stands, is unique in college history, and many eyes are watching with interest the development taking place here. (*La Torre*, 1929 p. [15])

In 1928 MacQuarrie's faculty was still rather small, numbering about 100 instructors, including the librarians. Sixty percent of the faculty were women. Typically, they possessed a master's degree in an academic specialization relating to schools and teaching. The Education and Teacher Training Department was the largest academic unit on campus, with 19 faculty members. The Physical Sciences Department was also quite large, with 16 faculty on staff. The Department of Librarianship was among the smallest units on campus. It had five faculty members in 1928, none of whom taught full time.

Although the college did not pursue big-name scholars until after World War II, San José State claimed several distinguished professors in 1928. James C. DeVoss, for example, was a well-published psychologist and chair of the Psychology Department. He had completed his doctoral work at Stanford University under the direction of Lewis

Terman, developer of the Stanford-Binet I.Q test. During the 1920s DeVoss and several other San José State professors teamed with Terman to conduct intelligence studies of immigrant and ethnic children in San José schools (Chapman, 1981).

Elmer Staffelbach was another well-known San José State faculty member closely tied to Stanford University. Before coming to San José State Staffelbach taught at Stanford and worked as a Hoover Institution research fellow. At San José State, he chaired the Education and Teacher Training Department and served as the California Department of Education's director of research. An outspoken advocate for the professionalization of education, Staffelbach wrote numerous texts and treatises, although he is best known as the editor of the *Stanford Speller.*

Henry Meade Bland was, perhaps, San José State's most acclaimed instructor in the 1920s. Hired in 1899, Bland was the college's first faculty member with a PhD, though his fame was not as a research scholar but as a gifted teacher and poet. During the 1928-1929 academic year, Bland chaired the English Department and was named California's Poet Laureate.

As San José State expanded its curricular programs in the 1920s, its student body grew and diversified. In 1920, the school had just 400 students. By fall of 1927, 1,538 students were enrolled in classes. More than two-thirds of the students were women, causing something of a housing crunch since there were no dormitories on campus (*Bulletin*, 1928-1929, p. 27). According to the 1928-1929 *Bulletin*, 50% of the women students lived in San José with their parents or other family members, while many others lived at home and commuted to school (p. 27). For those living independently, the college established an authorized list of student housing, stipulating that "no woman student away from home may live in any house unless it is on the approved list." San José State further insisted that women students "secure permission from the office of the Dean of Women before changing their residences at any time" (p. 27). Monthly rent ranged from $35 to $45, with an extra $10 charged for board and housekeeping. The 1929 student handbook indicated that although personal expenses varied, "there was no need for extravagant expenditures for either dress or recreation. On the contrary, real economy is encouraged" (p. 39).

Despite such personal restrictions, students enjoyed an active recreational and social life. There were more than 30 student organizations on campus, ranging from the Archery and Bel Canto Clubs to the Women's Athletic Association and the YWCA. The college sponsored a plethora of student publications, such as the *State College Times*, the *Spartan Spasms*, as well as the elegant senior yearbook, *La Torre*. San José State also had a long tradition of successful men's athletic teams. They enjoyed particular prowess during the 1928-1929 season, defeating archrival Chico State in both football and basketball and winning the California Coast Conference basketball championship as well (*La Torre*, 1929, p. 244). Women students did not participate in intercollegiate sports, but instead played in intramural leagues. Their teams pitted class against class with the goal of teaching female students "the value of co-operative group play" (*La Torre*, 1929, p. 266).

Nineteen twenty-eight happened to be a leap year, and San José State students had fun with the associated gender stereotypes throughout the year. "Asserting their independence," or so the yearbook said, women students masterminded a last-minute write-in campaign and elected a woman as student body president over two male opponents (*La Torre*, 1928, p. 196). Coeds also organized a series of Sadie Hawkins events, declaring February 29 "Woman's Day" and hosting a "Leap Year Frolic" that featured a "get your man" race composed of old maids, flappers, and man hunters (*La Torre*, 1928, p. 40). Given the college's focus on women students during the 1928-1929 academic year, how appropriate that the nation's new first lady—Lou Henry Hoover—was a San José State alumna.

San José State did not keep a record of its minority students in the 1920s. Not that there was much need since a cursory examination of student names and faces in the yearbooks revealed a student body that was almost entirely white.[4] No African American appeared in either the 1928 or 1929 yearbooks and only a handful of Asian Americans were pictured. An exception to the sea of white faces in San José State's yearbooks was the Filipino Club, with 24 members in 1928 and 34 members in 1929. Club president in both years was the strikingly handsome Eugene Custodio, who seemed to possess a high profile on campus.

[4] No ethnic names or faces appear among the faculty either.

The campus itself was maturing into an attractive and substantial educational setting. Washington Square had become a lush park filled with trees, flowerbeds, and a network of walkways. The mission-styled main building housed the college's administrative offices and the library, while most academic departments were located in separate structures arranged in a quadrangle. The campus focal point was an ivy-covered tower, which served as the college's anchor and enduring symbol. San José State in the late 1920s ran a "co-operative store," which supplied books, food, and classroom materials, and the "Edwin Markham Health Cottage,"[5] a facility that dispensed medical services. Staffed by a doctor and nurses, the cottage provided students with two weeks' worth of medical care for their $3 annual tuition.

The college library, located on the main building's ground floor, had been remodeled and expanded in 1927. The high-ceilinged, well-lighted main reading room held 25,000 books and seated 200 students. The room had cream-colored walls and a modern green cork carpet, which helped dampen the sound of voices and sliding chairs (Backus, 1929, p. 44). In 1930, the library separated its reference and circulation desks, creating for the first time two discrete units. An old-fashioned elevated "librarian's stand" had been removed earlier in response to librarians' complaint that it put "the attendant too much in the position of an 'overseer' and disciplinarian" (Backus, 1927/1928, Memorandum, SJSU Archives). It was replaced by a redesigned circulation desk equipped with book chutes and modern labor-saving devices.

Given San José's more recent library history, it's interesting that the San José Public Library was also located on the college campus and allowed students use of books and services. Then there was a third "training school library" that was used by students and local children. It contained about 3,000 children's books and other items commonly found in schools. Its purpose was to give students first-hand experience working with books and children.

In 1928, San José State employed six librarians: Joyce Backus, head librarian; Helen Bullock and Ruby Kerr, catalogers; Joy Belle Jackson

[5] Edwin Markham graduated from San Jose State Normal School in 1872. An educator and poet, Markham is best known for his poem "The Man With a Hoe" (1899).

and Caroline Hubbard Bailey assistant librarians; and Emelyn Beattie, head of the training school library. Other library employees were Edith Bond, who helped with circulation and reference, and Florence Keegan, who oversaw the reserve reading room.

San José State's librarians were in their late thirties and early forties, except for Joy Belle Jackson, who was 29, and Edith Bond, a 22-year-old student assistant. All were unmarried and, like their student counterparts, lived close to campus, either with family or in boarding houses abutting Washington Square. Joyce Backus, Helen Bullock, and Florence Keegan lived in the same residence on San Salvador Street. The head of the art department, Ruth Wooster, also had a room there. Edith Bond, who lived on San Antonio Street, had Gertrude Tucker, a Physical Training Department instructor, for a next-door neighbor. Living and working in such close proximity, many San José State librarians and faculty developed life-long friendships, attending professional meetings and vacationing together over the years.

The librarian with arguably the most interesting background was Caroline Hubbard Bailey. She was named after her paternal grandmother who, with her husband Edward, had migrated to Hawaii in the 1830s as teaching missionaries. The elder Baileys lived for the remainder of their lives in Maui, where Edward Bailey became a well-known naturalist and artist.[6] Caroline's father, Charles Alden Bailey, was born in Hawaii in 1850, but by 1890 had moved to Alhambra, California, where Caroline was born. She attended Mills College and received her professional training at the Riverside Library Service School. She then moved to Los Gatos, California, with her elderly parents, where she secured a position at the Los Gatos Public Library. In a letter written in 1920 to the Hawaiian Mission Children's Society (a group of former missionaries and their families), Caroline described her new professional life in Northern California:

> We've been in Los Gatos for over a year and like it very much—the hills at this time of year remind us of the Islands. For about three months I've been librarian here and I love it. It means a great deal to us all that I am

[6] The Bailey House is now a museum near Lahaina.

> able to be at home. While the work is by no means easy, much of it is pleasant and I meet many interesting people who come by for our scenery and climate. Daddy sends his aloha nui and mother her old-time aloha. (Hawaiian Mission Children's Society, 1920, p. 29)

Caroline was still living in Los Gatos with her widowed mother when the San José State College Library hired her in 1926.

The Department of Librarianship

The Department of Librarianship was one of four new degrees established by San José State in the fall of 1928. Interestingly, these new programs were in professions then dominated by women: librarianship, nursing, commerce, and speech and stage craft. While librarianship and nursing had long been considered female occupations, "commerce" focused on secretarial and accounting skills, jobs customarily handled by women at that time. Women were also prevalent in the movie industry in the 1920s and 1930s, working as producers, screenwriters, costume makers, and set designers (Mahar, 2006). San José State's keen interest in offering degrees of interest to women made sense, though, given the college's current demographics.[7]

The Department of Librarianship was not simply a gambit to appeal to its primarily female student body. Its value and need stemmed from important changes taking place in California schools and in the library profession. When the California State Normal School opened in San José in 1871, professional education in librarianship was nonexistent. It would be more than a decade before the nation's first program in "library economy" opened at Columbia University in 1887. The Los Angeles Public Library established California's earliest training program in 1891. Its aim was to prepare young women for work in that institution only. Other California public libraries developed similar apprenticeship programs. The Riverside Public Library Service

[7] This emphasis on women's occupations was short-lived. In 1930 San José State founded the nation's first college degree program in police science.

School was the largest and most enduring of these public library-based schools, operating from 1910 through 1943. The California State Library sponsored a library training program from 1914 until 1920, when it merged with the newly formed library science department at the University of California, Berkeley. These were the schools in existence in California when San José State Teachers College began teaching library courses in 1921.

As library training programs multiplied, the American Library Association (ALA) felt an increasing need to regulate their structure and content. In 1924 the ALA created the Board of Education for Librarianship (BEL) to develop professional educational standards and, based upon them, to accredit library training programs. Administered by Executive Secretary Sarah Bogle and her assistant, Anita Hostetter, the BEL produced ALA's first accrediting standards in July 1925. These standards recognized four different types of library training programs which, depending on the coursework taken, earned students either a professional certificate, a bachelor of arts, or a master of arts in librarianship. Using these new standards and accompanying guidelines, the ALA accredited 15 library schools between 1925 and 1930, including the program at the University of California, Berkeley (White, 1976).

However, the ALA was unclear about its role in accrediting school library training programs, since school librarians were already certified by state departments of education and local school boards. As a result, the BEL decided not to formally accredit school library programs, although in its 1925 standards it prescribed two possible approaches. The first was a one-year post-bachelor's certificate that prepared librarians for full-time work in schools. The second was a "teacher-librarian" track that integrated library science courses into a college's teacher-training curriculum for individuals interested in working in a school library a couple of periods each day.

In the 1920s, California public schools employed both types of school librarians, depending on the size of the school and its tax-based funding. For example, a survey of 371 high schools conducted by the American Library Association's Education Committee in 1928 found that all but six of the schools responding (70%) had some sort of library on the premises. In terms of staffing, 51% of these libraries were managed by a part-time teacher-librarian, while 41% employed a librarian full time. The survey also revealed that almost half (45%) of the persons working in high school libraries had no library science training, and 8% of the schools had "no designated" person responsible for the library at all. "It would seem that our school boards and principals," survey coordinator Daisy Lake wryly observed, "are more willing to buy the books than to pay for librarians trained to select, circulate and arouse an interest in them" (Lake, 1929, p. 75). A concurrent study of junior high schools had similar findings. Although all schools responding to the survey reported having some sort of library facility on the premises, only 42% of the "librarians" in charge met the state's new special credential requirements (Fullwood, 1929, p.70).

By surveying and reporting on school library staffing, librarians were making the strong point that the state of California needed some sort of college-based training program to meet the requirements of the newly adopted Special Credential in Librarianship. Many looked to San José State to fill that need.

Superintendent of Public Instruction Vierling Kersey sympathized with librarians' concern over the management of school libraries. An advocate of progressive school reform, Kersey considered school libraries imperative in teaching schoolchildren critical thinking skills and a love of learning. As he outlined in a speech delivered at the 1929 California Library Association meeting:

> Education is a multiple process now, and the teacher is no stronger than the materials at hand. . . . Self-teaching habits must be promoted to continue the learning process beyond the school age, and to do this the educator must tie up with the library; he must bring the pupil to realize that he can go to the library to continue his education. (California Library Association, 1929, p. 49)

Kersey also recognized that school librarianship was a separate teaching field requiring special education. This was the rationale behind creation of the Special Credential in Librarianship instituted in 1928. This belief also prompted Kersey to endorse San José State's fledgling

Department of Librarianship as the official agency to prepare students for that credential.

Conclusion

The 1920s was a transformative period in the history of San José State. Responding to educational changes inspired by the progressive movement, San José State rapidly evolved from a small, teacher-training school to a large, multidisciplinary educational institution. The Department of Librarianship was one of several new academic units created in 1928 as part of the college's expanding mission and goals. Over the next decade, the department would modernize and systematize its teacher-librarian training course and experiment with ways to permit employed teachers to earn a professional library degree. This creative and experimental outlook would become an enduring characteristic of library science education at San José State.

Chapter 2

Creating the Department of Librarianship, 1928-1929

> I am much encouraged over the tendency here at San Jose State to develop a personality of our own, paying little or no attention to the customs and traditions of any other college. I like to think of ourselves as a pioneering college and still pioneering. I doubt if we have made so much use of the fact that our traditions are rooted in the early history of California, and that if any college should show an independence of spirit and a tendency to blaze new trails, it should be San Jose State.

—Thomas MacQuarrie
President's Message
La Torre, 1930

The founding and early development of the School of Library and Information Science (SLIS) exemplifies the independent and pioneering spirit that Thomas MacQuarrie commended in 1930. Originally established to train school librarians, the program was inspired by California's progressive education movement of the 1920s that sought to make schooling more interactive and develop in children critical-thinking skills and the habit of life-long learning (Weiler, 1994). Libraries played an important part in this new educational philosophy, and increasingly, public schools sought to make books and other curricular material available to teachers and students. While most schools or school districts funded or provided access to a collection of books, there was a dire need for trained personnel to manage them. San José State stepped up to meet that need.

The first mention of a library science degree appears in an undated and unsigned memorandum, probably written in 1927 or 1928 by college librarian Joyce Backus. According to this communication, "consideration" was being given to developing coursework for school librarians, "with possibly some thought" toward educating young women for positions in county and municipal libraries ("San Jose," n.d., SJSU Archives). President MacQuarrie endorsed the plan in January 1928, and thereafter the Department of Librarianship began to take shape.

Library Director Backus hoped that the contemplated library science degree would "measure up" to the American Library Association's (ALA's) educational standards and be accredited by ALA's Board of Education for Librarianship (BEL) ("San Jose," n.d., SJSU Archives). As soon as she secured President MacQuarrie's approval, she contacted the BEL to inquire about the accreditation process (Backus to Bogle, 11 January 1928, ALA Archives). Sarah Bogle, the board's executive secretary, quickly obliged by sending Backus copies of the latest ALA accreditation standards and a related publication spelling out curriculum criteria for school librarianship.

At the same time, Bogle wrote to California State Librarian Milton Ferguson to learn more about this upstart library school:

> We have just received a letter from Miss Joyce Backus, Librarian of the State Teachers College of San Jose, California, stating that the State Board of Education has just granted to this college the power to grant an A.B. degree with a major in library science.
>
> We shall greatly appreciate any information which you can give us in regard to the State Teachers College and its standing in the state, and shall be glad to know your opinion as to the quality of the work in library science which would be offered there.

Lest Ferguson interpret her inquiry as prejudiced against the West Coast school, Bogle concluded on a more positive note:

> We have been hearing a great deal about the need of courses for the preparation of school librarians to meet the need in California and are greatly interested in doing whatever we can to encourage courses which will exactly fulfill this purpose. (Bogle to Ferguson, 24 January 1928, ALA Archives)

Ferguson responded that he had recommended to Backus that she obtain from the BEL "the advice and cooperation of the people most interested in this work." The state librarian affirmed that San José State had a "very good reputation" and delineated the college's strengths:

> It has an excellent faculty, is in rather close contact with Stanford University, is in a section of the state well equipped with libraries of various types for laboratory purposes, and I see no reason why it should not make a great success of an undergraduate library school. . . .

Ferguson also had positive things to say about Thomas MacQuarrie:

> The president of the college who is a recent appointee and I think a very alert man wants to put in the right sort of school for librarianship. His ambition is to train workers for school libraries and for the assistants in county and public libraries generally. It is not his aim to specialize in the executive field which presumably is more or less satisfactorily taken care of in California by the State University.

Ferguson concluded that while San José State was eager to develop this new school library degree, "it has everything yet to do" (Ferguson to Bogle, 27 January 1928, ALA Archives). The first step was to design the curriculum.

Curriculum

In developing a library science program to address California's growing need for professional librarians, Backus and her colleagues sought to create a curriculum suitable for school librarians but general enough for those interested in other types of library work. They also anticipated that students would enter the program with varying educational and professional backgrounds and therefore would need different degrees to meet their career interests. With these factors in mind, the department decided to offer three educational tracks:

1. Bachelor of arts degree leading to a joint teaching and librarianship credential;
2. Bachelor of arts degree with a librarianship major;
3. One-year post-graduate course in librarianship for students who already possessed a bachelor's degree or teaching credential.

In addition to these professional degrees, the department also instituted a junior-college vocational program for individuals seeking "minor positions in libraries" (*Bulletin,* 1928-1929, p. 108-111).

The original curriculum covered current library science methods, including cataloging, reference, library arts and crafts, library accounting, book appreciation, library history, and school library administration. Several courses were taught outside the Library Department, such as lettering and book crafts in the Art Department and children's literature in the Education Department. Students were also required to take a two-quarter internship called "Library Practice."

In designing this curriculum, the department tried to reflect ALA's 1925 educational standards while satisfying the criteria set forth in California's school librarianship credential. This was challenging, for although California's 1928 credential standards did not require that students take specific classes, they did stipulate that the coursework had to be taken from an ALA-accredited library school. Faced with this accreditation conundrum, Joyce Backus asked the BEL whether it was possible to be "tentatively" accredited and then granted "a year or so to build up our school" (Backus to Hostetter, 15 April 1929, ALA Archives). Anita Hostetter, BEL's assistant secretary, responded unequivocally: "No school is fully accredited until it has been in operation at least two years and has been visited by representatives of the board in two different years" (Hostetter to Backus, 24 April 1929, ALA Archives). Complicating matters further, President MacQuarrie was philosophically opposed to any interference by non-academic agencies outside of California. He therefore refused to support Backus's negotiations with the ALA regarding early accreditation.

Despite these unresolved issues, the Department of Librarianship was ready to start teaching classes in the fall of 1928. Accredited or not, Backus began recruiting faculty and students for the program's inaugural year.

Faculty

Traditionally library science education was conducted within a given college's library, with the library director serving as department chair and the college librarians as instructors. In the 1920s, San José State librarians enjoyed faculty status, so apparently there was no philosophical or administrative problem with their developing an academic program. Accordingly, Backus functioned as department chair, and four other librarians—Helen Bullock, Joy Belle Jackson, Ruby Kerr, and Emelyn Beattie—added teaching to their regular responsibilities. With professional degrees from some of the nation's premier library science programs and a broad range of work experience in school, public, and college libraries, these librarians designed the department's first course offerings. The department also enlisted the services of other instructors on campus as well as highly reputed staff in local libraries to complete the proposed schedule. This creative use of full- and part-time faculty would become a defining characteristic of San José State's library science program in the future.

Although data concerning SLIS's original faculty is decidedly limited, information gleaned from census records, professional publications, and institutional archives affords a glimpse into these women's personal and professional lives and hints at what they each contributed to the Library Department's development. Of course, the most important of these faculty members was the founding chair, Joyce Backus. Born in

Nebraska in 1895, she lived in Washington before earning a BS in library science from Boston's Simmons College. Graduating in 1920, her first professional position was in the Washington State Normal School library (now Central Washington University). Backus also worked for several years at the California State Library before accepting, in 1923, the head librarian position at San José State Teacher's College. Robert Gitler, who worked for Backus in the 1930s, described her as "a dedicated, brilliant Librarian/Administrator [with] the mind of a military strategist, yet with a quiet pixyish sense of humor." Many years later, Gitler vividly recalled Backus's tiny writing in perfect library hand, "an art she retained through her entire life and which in a way reflected the perfection of everything to which she applied herself" (Gitler, 1990, p. 2). Backus devoted her 30-year career at San José State to expanding and modernizing the college library and building up its library science program. When she resigned her position as department chair in 1950, over 200 librarians had her to thank for their professional degree.

Another important founding faculty member was Helen Bullock, who worked and taught at San José State for 35 years. Born in New York in 1892, she grew up in a prominent family in Canton, Pennsylvania, where her father practiced law and served on the local school and library boards. Bullock earned a certificate in library science from Syracuse University and worked in a series of professional positions before moving to San José. These jobs ranged from working in the New York Public Library to serving as public librarian in Lodi, California. Bullock spent several years in the mid-1920s employed at the University of Michigan library, while simultaneously earning a BA in English. Graduating from Michigan in 1927, Bullock spent brief stints as a branch librarian for the Los Angeles Public Library and as a Canton (PA) High School teacher, before coming to San José State in 1929. Aside from spending several summers in New York to earn a library science BS at Columbia University, Bullock remained in San José until her 1962 retirement. Her positions included senior librarian in charge of the reading room and head reference librarian. Although she taught a variety of library science courses, Bullock specialized in cataloging and classification.

The remaining founding faculty had shorter academic careers, quite possibly reflecting women's employment opportunities and correlated limitations in that era. Joy Belle Jackson, for example, taught for the department during its inaugural year, but soon left San José State to become the chief librarian for the Tuolumne County Library System. Born in 1899 and raised along Chicago's North Shore suburbs, Jackson attended Northwestern University and then moved to California, where she earned a bachelor's degree and a library science certificate from UC Berkeley. Jackson began her career in 1922 as a teacher at Petaluma Junior High School, and the following year she secured a position at the Santa Clara Free Library as head of the library's school department. In 1926, she came to San José State, where she ran the college's main library reading room and taught courses covering reference, bibliography, and the history of books. She left college library work about 1931 and spent the next three decades as a librarian in the California counties of Tuolumne, Yolo, and Alameda.

Born in Iowa in 1888, Ruby Kerr was the most senior of the original SLIS faculty. Her family moved in about 1910 to California, where Kerr earned a master's degree from Stanford University and a library science certificate from UC Berkeley. Presumably, she was a full-time teacher, for she did cataloging and other professional work for San José State's library during school vacations. During the 1928-1929 academic year, she taught library economy, the history of libraries, and library methods. The department's annual report indicates that Kerr suffered from an undisclosed illness, which ultimately forced her to leave the program. In 1930, she was teaching high school in San Francisco and no longer associated with San José State.

The last original faculty member was Emelyn Beattie, who was in charge of the training school library and taught children's services courses. Born in Ontario, Canada, in 1892, Beattie was raised in Campbell, California, where her father owned an orchard. At 18, she moved to Ogden, Utah, and there worked in its public library. During the summers she traveled to Pittsburgh, Pennsylvania, to attend the Carnegie Institute, which offered the first training program for children's librarians. In 1914, Beattie returned to San José and found work at the San José Public Library. Two years later, she took a job at the Santa Clara County Library, staying there until joining the San José State faculty in 1926. In keeping with the expectation of her generation, in 1930 Beattie gave up her library career to marry Easton Kent.

The Department of Librarianship supplemented its regular library-based faculty with part-time instructors drawn from other academic departments and nearby libraries. "We feel," explained Backus in one of her reports, "that it is better to have work given by several different people than by one full time instructor" ("Department of Librarianship," 1928/1929, SJSU Archives). The earliest SLIS part-timers were Arthur Caryl Kelley and Fjeril Hess. Although not professionally trained librarians, Kelley and Hess nonetheless possessed impressive credentials. Kelley taught accounting in the Commerce Department, an academic program which, like library science, was just getting started in 1928. With a master's degree from the University of Chicago, Kelley had been working as a federal tax auditor before accepting a teaching position at San José State. A serious scholar, Kelley's articles appeared in such academic periodicals as the *Journal of Political Economy* and the *Accounting Review.* He also published the *Essentials of Accounting* in 1935. For the Department of Librarianship, Kelley developed a course on library accounts and budgets.

Fjeril Hess taught courses in book appreciation and library history. Born in Omaha, she lived in Portland, New York City, Los Angeles, and Salt Lake City, moving frequently, as her father worked for the Union Pacific Railroad. Upon earning a BA in 1915 from MacMurray College in Illinois, Hess found her first teaching job at a ranch school in Nevada's Big Smoky Valley and then did foreign community work in Passaic, New Jersey. Hess left the US in 1919 for graduate study at the University of Prague. From 1922-1925, she was the managing editor of the *Woman's Press Magazine*. She began her two-decade literary career authoring works of non-fiction and drama in the mid-1920s, but earned true fame in the 1930s as a children's fiction writer specializing in multicultural themes.[8] While employed in her brother-in-law's San José bookstore, Hess taught for San José State during the summers of 1928-1930.

Finally, during its first academic year the Department of Librarianship enlisted the help of several Art Department instructors. Professor Susan Byrne, holder of a Columbia BA and MA, created a course on bookbinding, while Estelle Hoisholt, an alumna of San José

---

[8] Some of Hess's better-known works are *Buckeroo: A Story of a Piñon Camp* (1931), *The House of Many Tongues* (1935) *and Shanty Brook Lodge* (1937).

State Teachers College and Stanford University, offered "Lettering." Both Byrne and Hoisholt had taught for San José State since 1920.

The Department of Librarianship's founding faculty was a diverse lot with extensive professional experience and impressive academic credentials. Yet the fluidity and impermanence of the library's professional staff—a situation exacerbated, perhaps, by some disgruntlement with the increased workload—underscored the department's need to hire instructors experienced in and committed to library science education. In the coming decades, the necessity of differentiating between teaching faculty and library faculty would assume increasing importance.

Students

In her first departmental annual report, Joyce Backus declared that the library training program was off to "rather a promising start" with students "enthusiastic and interested in their work" ("Department of Librarianship," 1928/1929, SJSU Archives). This first library science cohort was purposely kept small, for Superintendent Kersey had not officially authorized the new degree at the semester's start. Admitted students had to have completed two years of college, demonstrate a reading knowledge of two modern languages, and be able to "typewrite accurately" (*Bulletin*, 1928-1929, p. 109). The department also accepted a few "special students," individuals who did not meet the academic prerequisites but were already working in libraries.

Twelve full-time and three part-time students enrolled in the library science program in its first year. Eleven of their names are known: Edna B. Williams, Benecia de Niedman, Hollis V. Knopf, Grace Laughton, Mildred Beymer, Adelyn Skonovd, Bernice Sheld, Marian Bambauer, Elizabeth Souther, Doris M. Garcelon, and Dorothy Wood. As with SLIS founding faculty, while biographical information about these original students is exceedingly thin, some general observations can still be made. Obviously, the entire student body was female; in fact, the Department of Librarianship would not attract a male student until the early 1950s. The average student's age was 27, though in actuality their ages varied widely. Hollis Knopf and Dorothy Wood were just 19, while Marian Bambauer, Mildred Beymer, Benecia de Niedman, and

Bernice Sheld were in their 20s. Several were substantially older: Grace Laughton was 34, Elizabeth Souther was 38, while Doris Garcelon and Edna Williams were both 40.

Although diverse in age, the students' personal backgrounds were quite similar to and typical of San José State's student body as a whole. All were white and American-born. Six were California natives, two were from Minnesota, and one each was from Missouri, Nebraska, and Illinois. The majority of their parents were American citizens, though only three hailed originally from California. Four students' parents were immigrants: De Niedman's father was Russian; Garcelon's parents were French Canadians; Sheld's father was Swedish; and Skonovd's father was Norwegian and her mother was Swedish.

SLIS's original students were also similar in socioeconomic background, with four of their fathers being farmers, one a dairyman, and another a railroad expressman. Grace Laughton's father was a clergyman. Only Benicia de Niedman appears to have been from a more affluent background, as her father was a U.S. Army officer and surgeon.

Most of the students' families were residing in California when their daughters launched their library science schooling, though not necessarily in the immediate San José area. Marian Bambauer lived in Pacific Grove, Mildred Beymer in Riverside, Doris Garcelon in Arcata, Hollis Knopf in Campbell, Grace Laughton in Tulare County, and Bernice Sheld in Stanislaus County. Moreover, at least eight of the original twelve students had attended San José State Teachers College before starting the library science program, whereas Edna Williams, Benecia de Niedman, Bernice Sheld, and Grace Laughton were currently enrolled in San José State's General Education credential program. Hollis Knopf, Marian Bambauer, and Dorothy Wood were in San José State's junior college program, while Adelyn Skonovd was seeking a Bachelor of Arts.

Interestingly, several of these SLIS pioneers were reentry students who had been teaching or rearing families and now came back to college to earn a professional library certificate or degree. Elizabeth Souther, for example, was 38 and working at the San José Public Library when she entered the program. Grace Laughton had been teaching near Modesto when, at age 34, she returned to San José State to study librarianship. She, along with Edna Williams, was married.

The other students' marital status is difficult to establish. However, records indicate that at least five—Edna Murphy Williams, Mildred Beymer Graham, Hollis Knopf Erickson, Grace Limmerick Laughton, and Adelyn Skonovd Lorraine—were married or got married soon after earning their degrees. Edna Murphy Williams had two children, while Grace Laughton headed a household that included her mother and two nieces.

What happened to these students professionally? Of the original dozen students, at least six graduated in 1930. Most others completed their degrees the following year. Seven of these alumnae continued to appear in the professional literature over the years, mostly working within a school or academic environment in California. Hollis Knopf became a librarian at Marin Junior College. Grace Laughton was a teacher-librarian in the Fresno County School System. Mildred Beymer worked at Roosevelt High School in San Francisco, while Marian Bambauer taught at the grammar school in Saratoga. Doris Garcelon, whose family resided in Arcata, landed a job at nearby Humboldt State College library. A few of the graduates found jobs in California's public and county libraries. In 1930, for instance, Elizabeth Souther was still living in San José and working at the city's public library, while Dorothy Wood was employed in the Plumas County Library. In the 1940s, Doris Garcelon moved to San Luis Obispo and there also became a public librarian.

When viewed as a whole, the demography of SLIS's first class closely parallels that of today's student body. Typically, they were from a white, middle-class background, though almost half were from immigrant families. Most were re-entry students seeking a new career in libraries or professional education to enhance their current library positions. Many were older than typical college students, and at least five were married or would get married soon after graduation. Upon graduation, they commonly found jobs as school librarians or academic librarians, reflecting the curricular emphasis of San José's program. As far as those already employed in library positions, they continued in the same institution during attendance at and even after graduation from San José State.

Summer School

In the summer of 1929, the Department of Librarianship inaugurated a summer school course that dramatically expanded the school's influence in California libraries. Since the turn of the century, library schools throughout the US had been offering summer institutes to provide professional training for working librarians unable to enroll in classes during the regular academic year. Indeed, summer school programs were so prevalent in library science education that the Board of Education for Librarianship developed a separate set of educational standards for summer schools and maintained an official list of accredited programs. Because San José State had operated a successful summer program for working teachers since 1903, the Library Department's summer courses were part of an established on-campus enterprise (Walsh, 2006, p. 28).

The department's summer program was designed for "experienced teachers, librarians and others interested in school or children's library work" (Summer School Announcement, 1929, ALA Archives). Admission requirements were purposely relaxed to encourage individuals already working in libraries or teachers assigned library responsibilities to enroll in classes. Predictably, most summer school students were already employed as teachers and public librarians, and they returned to their regular jobs once summer courses were completed. Only students seeking the professional degree applied for admission to the college. If accepted, they could complete their library certificate over the course of four or five summers.

For many years, summer school was the department's most successful and ambitious educational achievement, attracting students from all over California and beyond. In 1929, for example, 32 students from three states (California, Nevada, and Washington) were enrolled. They had a choice of six classes: reference, cataloging, library practice, children's literature, school libraries, and book arts. Although couched in lofty objectives, practically speaking, summer school was a welcome generator of revenue and resources. Classes were self-funded, requiring students to pay $15 per course as compared to the $3 fee charged during the regular academic semester.

Since summer teaching was voluntary for regular library faculty, student fees paid their salaries. Usually one or two of the college librarians taught in the summer, which helped supplement their income. The department then hired "visiting faculty" to fill in the gaps, and thereby added variety and vitality to the school's course offerings. Indeed, often visiting faculty were (or would soon become) prominent librarians, library educators, children's authors, and, in later years, information scientists.

The department's 1929 summer school hired three visiting faculty: a Mrs. Fourtaine, who taught lettering; and two local librarians, Margaret V. Girdner and Wilhelmina Harper. While Fourtaine's background and position are unknown, Girdner and Harper were well respected in local professional circles. The daughter of a railroad watchman, Girdner spent her childhood in Butte, California, before earning a BA at Stanford in 1915 and a library degree at Berkeley in 1916. Girdner's regular job was as a high school librarian until 1933 when the San Francisco City School District hired her as an administrator.

Influential in the California Library Association (CLA) and the California School Library Association, Girdner published and lectured frequently on school library topics. At the 1929 CLA annual meeting, she gave a presentation titled, "School Library Visions," in which she warned of a new "Morrison plan" intended to supplant existing school libraries with a small collection of books in each classroom. Girdner forcefully argued that every school needed a trained school librarian to supervise all instructional materials. As the only teacher who "comes into direct content with every pupil" she advocated that the teacher-librarian become a "real directing force" in the schools (Girdner, 1929, pp. 86-87). That summer, Girdner taught two courses for San José State: Reference and Bibliography and School Libraries and Library Work with Children.

The department's first summer session also enlisted the services of Wilhelmina Harper, still another local librarian. Born in Farmington, Maine, in 1884, she earned degrees from Columbia's Teacher's College and the New York State Library School, and enjoyed a 35-year professional career that began in 1908 as a children's librarian in New York's Queens Borough Public Library. Her life took an interesting twist in 1918 when she became a library assistant at the Pelham Bay Naval Training Station and then, a year later, moved to Brest, France, to be a YMCA library organizer. In 1920, she came back to the US to work for the American Red Cross in Chicago. The next year, she returned to public librarianship in California, working in the Bakersfield and Redwood City libraries until her 1954 retirement. In 1929, Harper was working in Redwood City when she taught a summer-school course in children's literature and storytelling. Harper was an ideal choice to develop this course, for she had already published several children's books as well as a sourcebook for storytelling. Like her contemporary Fjeril Hess, Harper achieved fame as a children's author in the 1930s and 1940s, during which time she published over 40 compilations of stories for children and young adults.

Conclusion

During its first academic year, the Department of Librarianship's distinctive approach to professional education coalesced. Designed and implemented by the college librarians, the department's offerings were varied and flexible enough to appeal to the diverse interests and ambitions of prospective students. Although specializing in school librarianship, the initial coursework was sufficiently broad to appeal to individuals interested in other library employment. Students also were given a choice of degree options, ranging from paraprofessional training to a post-graduate certificate. The department was equally creative with its admissions requirements so that older, married, and working women still might pursue a professional degree. And although the library staff taught many of the initial courses, the department took advantage of outside expertise, hiring part-time instructors from other campus departments and the local library community. Pronouncedly entrepreneurial, the department used summer school sessions to expand its student and faculty base and supplement its modest budget. Guided by an intrepid department chair who skillfully navigated the dangerous waters of accreditation and college bureaucracy, the library science program moved into the next stage of its development with much hope and increasing confidence.

Chapter 3

Educating Teacher-Librarians, 1929-1945

> The new education needs the service of the library teacher who can teach children to use printed material efficiently. In the past we have been too afraid that some teacher untrained in the essentials of librarianship would enter our field of work; we should have been afraid that we who know about librarianship should fail as teachers. School librarianship is a big responsibility. Let's all be "library teachers!"
>
> —Mildred L. Beymer
> Class of 1930[9]

Throughout its history, the School of Library and Information Science (SLIS) prided itself in blazing new trails in professional education to meet the ever-changing needs of its key constituencies. Primary among these constituencies has been the American Library Association (ALA), which, via the Board of Education for Librarianship (BEL) and later the Committee on Accreditation, continued to upgrade and delineate standards for professional education. Locally, the California Library Association, California School Library Association, and other professional organizations promoted SLIS's development through

[9] Beymer, M. (1933, October). What's in a name? Editorial comments. *CSLA Bulletin, 6* (1), 9.

various committees, advisory groups, and collaborations. Full-time and part-time SLIS faculty also had an important impact upon the library school, as they reworked and redefined the curriculum to reflect their individual scholarly and professional interests and changes in the field. Students, too, influenced the direction of the school through their course selections, extracurricular activities, and experiences in the job market. Finally, and ultimately most important, the evolving nature of libraries and the library profession necessitated SLIS's continual experimentation with the content and delivery of its professional education.

San José State's early interest in developing a library science degree derived from a historic shift in California's educational system during the 1920s. Progressive educational methods, inspired by John Dewey and his followers, emphasized and sought to cultivate the individual talents of the state's schoolchildren to prepare them for productive and rewarding lives. This new educational philosophy was a boon for school libraries, which educators and administrators considered essential for developing in children the habit of self-learning. As the number of and educational uses for school libraries expanded, so did the need for teachers trained in library administration.

California state law required school districts to fund some sort of school library, at least at the district level. In some regions, the district's school board was responsible for creating and administering library materials and services for its constituent schools. Elsewhere school districts contracted with their counties to create "classroom libraries" as part of the county library branch system. Larger municipal libraries also worked with local schools, developing collections and outreach services for classroom teachers. The advantage of the county library and public library arrangement was that professional librarians, as opposed to elected school board members, selected books and managed library services for schools. The disadvantage, however, was that librarian visits to the schools were rare. And while trained in children's materials and services, public librarians were not teachers and, therefore, not professionally prepared to participate in curriculum development (Hall, 1974).

In the 1920s, county and city library systems discontinued their "school deposit service," and local schools assumed responsibility for classroom books and other teaching materials. Some districts expected individual teachers to be responsible for classroom collections, thus increasing the pressure on them to learn more about children's books and curriculum materials. Other districts appointed several teachers to devote one or two periods a day to manage the school library and assist other teachers with their classroom books. A few schools hired a specially trained teacher-librarian as a full-time manager of curricular materials. In 1928, the California Department of Education mandated that a teacher working in the library more than two periods a day possess both a teaching certificate and a special credential in school librarianship. The special credential in librarianship required that the library coursework be taken from an ALA-accredited library school. This was the professional/educational climate within which San José State's Department of Librarianship evolved.

Curriculum

Joyce Backus, San José State's Department of Librarianship chair, approached the task of designing a library science curriculum conscientiously and strategically. Knowing that the new degree program must be accredited to qualify students for California's school librarian positions, she secured from the ALA's Board of Education for Librarianship two important documents: Standards for a Junior Library School and Standards for the Training of School Librarians. While not binding, ALA's standards recognized two types of educational tracks for school librarians. The first track was designed to educate individuals already possessing a bachelor's degree who sought a one-year post-graduate certificate for full-time professional library work. The second track was for teacher-librarians, who took undergraduate library science courses as part of their teacher-training program. San José State's original library science curriculum supported both tracks. However, the teacher-librarian model predominated.

As noted earlier, the department's initial coursework consisted of twelve classes, ten required and two elective. The elective courses allowed students to specialize in either school libraries or children's work in public libraries. Students in the undergraduate teacher-librarian track took five to ten library science classes depending on whether they sought a major or minor in librarianship. The remaining classes were taken in the Education and English Departments. Although the Department of Librarianship also taught "library craft" courses—including lettering and book binding—in the junior college, this paraprofessional program was entirely separate from the BA and credential degrees.

Curricular development during the 1930s and 1940s was almost entirely motivated by the dictates of the ALA as the department worked toward accreditation. Backus was in regular contact with Sarah Bogle, director of the Board of Education for Librarianship, as she endeavored to meet ALA's standards while respecting the desires and goals of campus administrators. As part of the early accreditation process, Bogle came to San José State in January 1930 to survey the college's facilities and visit nearby libraries. She also met with President Thomas MacQuarrie, Superintendent Vierling Kersey, and several key faculty members (including Psychology Department Chair James de Voss) to discuss ALA requirements and expectations.

Although Bogle's meetings and social engagements were cordial, an incident with the local newspaper undermined the good impression Backus was trying to make. The *San Jose Mercury* covered the ALA executive's visit and reported that Bogle was quite impressed with the college's new library science program. "The proper training in the course is an important one," Bogle was quoted as saying, and "the methods used in San Jose will not only be copied by other schools in California, but throughout the United States" ("Local College Lauded," 1930). Unfortunately, Bogle had never spoken with this reporter and the news report was entirely fabricated. Bogle sent a telegram to the *Mercury* editor insisting that her purported praise be retracted. "I made no such statement nor any other on [the] subject. I shall appreciate your prompt action" (Bogle, Western Union, n.d., ALA Archives). Bogle also contacted President MacQuarrie about the "false interview" reported in the *Mercury*, commenting, "I felt sure you would want to correct the matter" (Bogle to MacQuarrie, 10 February 1930, ALA Archives). According to Backus, MacQuarrie felt that contacting the editor would be futile and thus he didn't bother (Backus to Bogle, 6 February 1930, ALA Archives).

Despite this embarrassing postscript, Bogle enjoyed her time in San José and provided Backus with helpful advice on the content and administration of the new library science program. Backus quickly reworked her original curriculum outline and resubmitted it to Bogle in early May (Backus to Bogle, 10 May 1930, ALA Archives). The revised curriculum did not change much in outward appearance, but course objectives and descriptions had a much stronger professional tone, and a clearer distinction was made between classes that taught students how to use library materials and those that focused on their management. For example, Book Appreciation was replaced with three courses on Book Selection. Reference and Bibliography changed from a course that gave students research experience to one based on the "critical examination" of reference sources and the criteria used for their selection. Cataloging, likewise, went from a "general course in simplified cataloging" to one that studied the "fundamental principles" of "ALA catalog rules" and other professional standards of the day. Finally, the department divided LIB 109 (School Libraries and Work with Children) into two separate courses to better distinguish between the school library and public library environments.

The BEL's assistant secretary, Anita Hostetter, scrutinized the revised curriculum against the 1925 accreditation standards. While she found that the redesigned classes came closer to meeting ALA guidelines, she worried over the extent to which certain topics were or were not covered and did not like that some courses, like children's literature, were taught in other academic departments. Hostetter also objected to the Department of Librarianship running a parallel paraprofessional program in the junior college, lest students and employers confuse the two. Expressing concern in a letter to her superior, Sarah Bogle, Hostetter argued that San José State's technical degree in library craft would adversely affect the professional character of courses in the other group (Hostetter to Bogle, 19 May 1930, ALA Archives).

Anxious to deflect ALA criticism away from the library science degree program, San José State eliminated the junior college courses in 1939. This move was also pragmatic, for the program in library craft was never particularly successful at getting students jobs. In a 1932 letter to Hope Smith of the Los Angeles Public Library, Backus surmised that because paraprofessional positions paid so poorly, libraries "did not look outside of their own community for applicants" (Parker, 1974, p.24). Furthermore, these jobs traditionally went to local girls whose personal connections and cultural credentials were more important than academic preparation. Recognizing this employment reality, the Department of Librarianship concentrated on professional education from that point forward.

As its curriculum evolved in the 1930s, the department adopted an educational philosophy that shaped its curricular focus well into the following decade. Although the faculty agreed that a school librarian should be "highly qualified in her profession of librarianship," they believed that her most important role was as a "master teacher" who specialized in children's books and their use. In the "progressive" school, Backus wrote in the *Western Journal of Education* in 1938, teachers and librarians had the "same objectives." Their work differed "in emphasis" only (pp. 10-11).

San José State's library science curriculum thus continued to be integrated into the School of Education with library courses taught as a subject major or minor. Coursework revolved around two main areas: collection development and school library management. In 1933, there were no less than six separate courses in book selection, each focusing on a specific subject area (e.g., history, biography, poetry, social science). The library department also increased the number of courses devoted to school libraries by adding Book Selection for School Libraries and Teaching the Use of Books and Libraries. In 1936, two more school-oriented classes were created: The School Library and School Library Administration.

The Department of Librarianship would specialize in educating teacher-librarians throughout the 1940s. Even when the department developed its first master's-level degree in 1954, the MA focused on school librarianship only. This school library emphasis served an important curricular role in the state's educational system by allowing California's other library schools to offer more comprehensive, professional degrees. However, it proved a liability when it came to San José State achieving ALA accreditation.

Accreditation

Despite the Department of Librarianship's steady development during the 1930s and 1940s, San José State did not pursue official ALA accreditation. Backus confided to Anita Hostetter in 1943 that although the faculty "always regretted" this inaction, President MacQuarrie "was uninterested in accrediting by out-of-state agencies." Backus also admitted that "there was pressure from outside groups who insisted that the state college was established and financed to serve state needs," which prevented the department from working more closely with the ALA (Backus to Hostetter, 3 March 1943, ALA Archives).

Despite MacQuarrie's convictions, the department faculty endeavored to change his mind. As early as 1932, Backus raised the issue in light of library school staffing. In a memo to the president regarding the department's need for a full-time faculty member, Backus wrote, "We cannot expect to be accredited by A. L. A. as long as we continue on the part-time basis" (8 February 1932, SJSU Archives). Backus tried again in 1936, requesting that the BEL send MacQuarrie "information and directions and necessary blanks for application for the accrediting of this department as an undergraduate school for the training of school librarians" (Backus to Hostetter, 13 May 1936, ALA Archives). Within a week Hostetter, now serving as BEL's executive secretary, sent the president accreditation materials along with an informative letter outlining the accreditation process. According to the ALA's records, MacQuarrie never responded (Summary of relations . . . with San Jose State College, 22 January, 1937, ALA Archives).

Ever hopeful, faculty member Jeannette Vander Ploeg visited ALA headquarters in Chicago in 1938, again to consult with Hostetter regarding accreditation. Here, the concern was ALA's stipulation that an accredited library school must have a departmental library for student use. At that meeting, Vander Ploeg reminded the ALA that "the president is opposed to regulation or standardization by any organization, national or state." Yet apparently, MacQuarrie had read an article in the ALA *Bulletin* regarding accreditation requirements and remonstrated "that if a training school library is insisted upon San José would not even consider requesting accreditation" (Vinton Memorandum, 22 August 1938, ALA Archives). Quickly jumping on

MacQuarrie's mere mention of accreditation, Vander Ploeg was able to secure from the ALA a statement that the departmental library requirement might be waived in this situation. Again, no response from MacQuarrie was forthcoming.

In addition to these accreditation concerns, the department also had to contend with the troublesome issue of professional status and the recognition of librarians as legitimate faculty. Although always included among college faculty in the annual yearbook, librarians carried a double load, teaching library science classes and shouldering regular professional responsibilities in the library. In a 1937 letter to MacQuarrie, Backus complained that salaries were too low. "Librarians are required to have as much academic and professional experience as faculty members," she argued, and their work is "an intrinsic part of the instructional program." She urged that librarians' salaries should equal the "salaries paid to faculty members of corresponding preparation and experience" (Backus to MacQuarrie, 4 March 1937, SJSU Archives).

Another threat to the department was ALA's push (supported by professional associations) to make library education exclusively a post-graduate degree. In May 1941, the State Department of Education addressed the proposition that the special credential in school librarianship require a graduate degree. The agency ruled against it, a decision that MacQuarrie supported. Indeed, in an article that appeared in the *Spartan Daily*, MacQuarrie warned that had this proposal been approved, "the library school here would have been done away with" ("Librarians Need Not Take Graduate Work," 1941).

Faculty

Despite continuing concerns over the department's accreditation and long-term prospects, the library science program was able to secure several new faculty members in the 1930s and 1940s who advocated for the important role of teacher-librarians in public schools. Margaret V. Girdner, for example, continued to teach for San José State in the 1930s, and her professional writings extolled the teacher-librarian model. "Some school libraries are merely small public libraries within the walls of the curriculum," she wrote in 1930, "and this is a natural outcome of the fact that the first school libraries were merely an extension of public library service within schools" (p. 113). But, she argued, the school library was distinct from children's work done in public libraries and, therefore, required different professional training. In her eyes, the "modern" school library should be considered a "teaching department" and run by a teacher-librarian "fully equipped in both library and teaching technique" (p. 115).

New faculty hired in the 1930s held similar views. Dora Smith, recruited as the department's first faculty member in 1930, was well known in professional circles for her advocacy of children's reading. Born in Utah in 1892, Smith began working in libraries at 18, earning a master of library science from UC Berkeley the year she was hired at San José State. Smith taught many courses for the department, including reference, bibliography, library administration, and promoting library use. She was active in professional organizations, using them as a platform to promote children's literature in elementary and high school curriculum. She argued that a properly educated teacher-librarian could, and should, serve as a guide to both teachers and students in their selection and use of books (Smith, 1938, p. 1035).

San José State recruited several other permanent faculty members in the 1930s to teach with Smith. The most important was Jeannette Vander Ploeg, or "Miss Van" as she was popularly known. A University of Illinois library school graduate, Vander Ploeg spent 27 years in the Department of Librarianship, teaching courses in cataloging and classification, library methods, bibliography, government publications, and technical processes. Another early faculty member was Frances Hichborn Purser, who was a San José State graduate. Receiving her library degree from UC Berkeley in 1929, San José State hired her as reference librarian and instructor in 1931. During her six years teaching for the college, Purser focused on library work with children as well as the undergraduate course called Use of Books and Libraries. Purser was rare among SLIS faculty at that time: she married in 1933 and continued working, at least until 1936 or 1937, when she moved to Alaska with her husband, a water conservation engineer. The *San Jose Mercury* featured the Pursers in a December 7, 1938, article with photographs of Frances in front of a primitive cabin with her team of sled dogs.

An interesting feature of San José State's early library science faculty was its incubation of new instructors who went on to become prominent educators in other institutions. Laura K. Martin, for example, began teaching for San José in 1938, covering courses in book selection, work with children, and school libraries. Born in Springfield, South Dakota, in 1906, Martin earned degrees from UCLA and Stanford, as well as completing graduate work in library science at the University of Chicago in the summers of 1938 and 1942. During the 1938-1939 academic year, she replaced Joyce Backus as the department head, while Backus did postgraduate work at Stanford. Martin left San José State in 1940 to accept a faculty position at the University of Kentucky. During a long, distinguished academic career at Kentucky, she published widely and served as the first president of the American Association of School Librarians.

The first PhD on SLIS's faculty was Hazel Pulling, who, like Laura Martin, joined the library staff and teaching faculty in 1938. A Canadian, Dr. Pulling did her undergraduate and graduate work at the University of Chicago before earning her BS in library science and PhD in history from the University of Southern California. While at San José, Pulling taught courses in book appreciation and book selection, before moving back to USC to become part of the faculty in the library science program started there in 1936. Pulling also did teaching stints at Florida State University, Texas Woman's University, and Immaculate Heart College, before retiring in 1965. In addition to contributing to the literature on library science and related topics, she also wrote extensively on Southern California history.

Elizabeth Groves, another Canadian among the department's early faculty, was a graduate of the University of British Columbia (BA) and the University of Washington (BS). She worked in school libraries before coming to San José State in 1942 to manage the education reading room. She also taught courses in children's literature and library work with children until she left the department to join the University of Washington faculty in 1945. Groves, too, became quite prominent after leaving San José State, serving as children's book editor for *Booklist* and chairing ALA's Newbery-Caldecott Committee in 1946. Her academic career was cut short, however, when she married in 1955, as the University of Washington then had a policy mandating that female library employees must be unmarried.

The most memorable of these faculty sojourners was Robert Gitler, whose distinguished career spanned many decades. The son of Russian immigrants, Gitler was born in New York City in 1905. Upon completing a BA in history and political science from UC Berkeley in 1931, he was hired by San José State library to run the library circulation department, a position he held while earning library science degrees at Berkeley (1937) and Columbia (1939). Gitler was the first male Backus hired to work in the library and to teach in the Department of Librarianship. "It was a period of some months," he later conceded, "before real compatibility and mutual understanding was developed" (Gitler, 1990, p. 2). In addition to managing students at the circulation desk, Gitler handled unwanted library visitors as well. When asked by a student reporter what might be lurking in the building's odd corners, Gitler replied, "most anything," and proceeded to provide examples. "For instance, there was that snake I caught on the downstairs steps. And those hump-backed mice (kangaroo mice) that live in the ventilators. Why, one day . . . but you mustn't publish that!" (*Spartan Daily*, 1 July 1941). In 1936, Gitler began teaching for the department, specializing in book appreciation and library methods. Gitler also developed the Legal and Police Bibliography course, which he taught in the college's pioneering police science program.

Gitler left San José in 1942 to join the U.S. Navy, serving the country until the war's end. Upon returning to civilian life in 1945, he was appointed director of the University of Washington Library and also assumed responsibility for its library school, as was the custom at that time. In 1950, Gitler was asked by the ALA to establish a library school at Keio University in Japan as part of the American postwar reconstruction effort. His extraordinary experience in Japan was documented by Michael Buckland in *Robert Gitler and the Japan Library School: An Autobiographical Memoir* (1999). In 1953, Gitler returned to the US to become the director of ALA's Board of Education for Librarianship. He later served as director of the library schools at the State University of New York at Geneseo and Peabody College.

During his long and eventful career, Gitler remained a faithful and valuable friend to San José State's Department of Librarianship. Despite his rocky start, he enjoyed a close friendship with Joyce Backus and expressed respect and appreciation for her hidden kindness. "It was not generally known," he wrote in a tribute to his former boss upon her death, "but Joyce Backus was very generous in financially assisting students who needed funds. And she delighted in being an 'irritant,' so to speak, in urging her young staff members to work for higher degrees, to advance professionally" (Gitler, 1990, p. 2). As previously noted, Gitler had earned degrees from Berkeley and Columbia while employed at San José State, and he credited Backus with making possible his "exciting careers" in "academic library administration and education" (p. 2).

In addition to this interesting group of regular San José State faculty, the department hired several prominent part-time instructors whose impressive credentials added immeasurably to the college's stature as a training program for teacher-librarians. The most famous part-timer was Doris Gates, who taught children's literature classes at San José State from 1940 to 1943. Born in nearby Mountain View in 1901, Gates was a children's librarian in the Fresno County Library until she resigned in 1940 to pursue writing and lecturing full time. Gates published numerous children's books over the next two decades and won several prestigious awards including a Newbery Honor for *Blue Willow* in 1941 and the William Allen White Children's Book Award for *Little Vic* in 1954.

During its first two decades, the Department of Librarianship was enriched by its faculty, all of whom—including the permanent faculty members—were working librarians. These individuals were well-versed in the educational theories in vogue at the time and endeavored to instill in students a love of books and the ability to impart that love to others.

Students

Despite its interesting faculty and classes, the department's student body remained quite small throughout the 1930s and early 1940s. In fact, in some years only one or two students graduated from the program. The decline in library science majors reflected deeper problems in the state's economy and limited prospects for aspiring librarians of all sorts. The California Library Association's 1932 annual report gave voice to the grave employment situation facing recent library school graduates. Edith Coulter, chair of the Library Schools Committee, estimated that by summer there would be 130 unemployed librarians in the state and warned that the situation would only get worse. "With the curtailment of library budgets," Coulter pessimistically wrote,

> No positions are being created and many libraries are forced to adopt the policy of not filling vacancies, others are actually dismissing assistants. These conditions pertain to all types of institutions, including school libraries. It is not an affair of this year or next, but probably of a decade. (Coulter, 1932, p. 63)

Students in San José State's Department of Librarianship ranged from seven to ten during the 1930s. This number dropped even further during World War II as the nation's manpower—and woman power—were siphoned off in support of the war effort. Faculty member Dora Smith recalled that campus administrators were "very kind and very nice to the Department" during the downturn, allowing it to continue "because we felt that there was a need for it. It was strange to have one student, but I did" (Parker, 1974, p. 25). Other California library schools were suffering similar student losses. UC Berkeley's department went on what it called a "war schedule," which meant it did not teach courses during the spring quarter. Los Angeles Public Library's training school had closed in 1932, while the program at Riverside Public Library was disbanded in 1943.

Modest though the department's student body was, they were active in school affairs and developed a busy social and academic calendar. In a report Joyce Backus submitted to the ALA in 1943, she emphasized how engaged her students were in campus life, indicating that "all of the seniors have held offices in campus organizations. Two play the piano, two have sung in a cappello [sic] choirs" (Library School Report, 1943, p. 3, ALA Archives). Backus's Library Log contains numerous entries regarding other student activities, such as a "Bibs Committee Meeting" (May 20, 1942), a "Bibs Picnic" (May 22, 1942), and a "Bibs Party" (February 5, 1943). "Bibs" was the nickname for the Bibliophiles, the department's student association. Organized in 1930, the Bibliophiles was open to students majoring or minoring in librarianship. According to the 1933 college yearbook, its purpose was twofold: "It provides social contacts between students and faculty, and furthers professional interest through talks by members of the staff at semi-weekly teas" (*La Torre,* 1933, p. 110). In addition to hosting social functions, the group contributed to various causes of the day. For example, in 1940, the Bibliophiles helped raise funds for the nationwide Children's Crusade to benefit European war refugees and promote peace.

Library science students formed a second group in the 1930s, the Iota Chapter of Alpha Beta Alpha, a national library science professional fraternity. Unfortunately, no records of this short-lived organization remain.

Most students were full time and fit the traditional demographics of San José State. Although the library science majors continued to be entirely female and presumably of white ethnic background, Joyce Backus reported in 1943 that contrary to the college's policy, the department had admitted three disabled students. One was already working as a librarian and her employer made a written plea that an exception to school policy be made in her case. Another had been sponsored by the State Department of Vocational Rehabilitation, and the third had submitted evidence and credentials demonstrating "marked ability" (Library School Report, 1943, p. 6b, ALA Archives).

Most students were also California residents and remained in the state after graduation. A survey of graduates conducted in 1943 revealed that 85% continued to reside in Northern California after graduation, 9% relocated to Southern California, and the remainder lived out of state. The same survey showed that of 112 individuals who responded to the survey, 40 were working in school libraries, 15 in public libraries, 8 in college libraries, and 3 in county or state libraries. Only 8 alumni indicated they were working in non-library positions. Thirty responded that they were "married, no longer working" (Library School Report, 1943, n.p., ALA Archives).

In 1945, the first person of color appeared among the traditionally white Bibliophiles. A photograph in that year's *La Torre* shows an attractive young African American woman in a checked dress identified as Versa Pittman. Although this is the only evidence of

Pittman's time in the program,[10] her breaking of the color barrier helped other minority students enter the program in the years to come.

Although their numbers were few, by the early 1940s the San José alumni were already achieving professional recognition and success. For example, Geraldine Nurney ('31) was appointed head of San José Public Library in 1943, a position she held until 1970. Elizabeth Blakey ('36) had moved East and was Supervisor of Library Projects for the Works Progress Administration. Beryl Hoskins ('38) enjoyed a 36-year career at Santa Clara University. Another 1938 graduate, Carolyn Mott, authored several important texts on children's librarianship in the late 1930s. *The Children's Book on How to Use Books and Libraries,* which she coauthored with Leo Baisden in 1937, was in continuous publication for over 30 years. Mott and Baisden co-wrote several other books together in the 1940s, including one with San José State instructor Gertrude Memmler (Nunes) titled *Books, Libraries and You* (1941).

Summer School

Compared to the size of the department's regular program, its summer school was wildly successful. Advertised in local newspapers and professional publications, San José State's summer courses attracted individuals already working in libraries who sought professional training though not necessarily a credential or college degree. As an advertisement placed in the March 1936 CLA *Bulletin* explained, the curriculum was "planned especially for the teacher who wishes to know more about the use of books in the new curriculum, and the teacher-librarian who wishes simple library technique" (p.14).

With the focus on teachers and teacher-librarians, San José State's summer courses centered on school library administration and children's reading, though the department always offered a selection of basic

[10] The California Death Index includes a record for a Versa Pittman, who died in Los Angeles on 25 January 1953. Born in Oklahoma in 1922, this unmarried woman was only 31 when she passed away. Perhaps this is what became of the department's first black student.

courses, including reference, bibliography, and cataloging for those individuals seeking a professional degree. Students could supplement these courses with summer school classes taught in other departments. For example, in 1936, students could choose from an eclectic mix of recommended classes, including puppetry, toy making, personal investment, and social hygiene, while in 1941 offerings ranged from flower arranging to current social movements.

Summer courses had no state funding, so tuition was steep. Yet in most years, 40 or more students enrolled in one or both summer school sessions. The department had minimal placement concerns, for as Backus wrote in her 1932 ALA report, the majority of summer students were "from permanent positions" (Summer Courses, 1932, p. 2, ALA Archives). And although the department imposed no admissions requirements, it was expected that students had a minimum of two years of college before attempting the coursework.

Since regular faculty were not required to teach in the summer, the department hired notable part-time faculty to cover the courses. Summer students benefited from courses taught by Margaret Girdner and Doris Gates. Another interesting summer faculty member was Bess Landfear, who worked with Girdner as visual aids librarian for the San Francisco School District. Landfear was extremely active in the state's professional associations and published regularly on the latest technologies for school libraries (Landfear, 1940, p. 12). Margaret Oldfather was another summer instructor. Employed for the 1930 session, she was the head of cataloging at Ohio State University's library, and during her 40-year library career became a respected authority in cataloging and classification.

It was a real coup in 1936 when Gladys Potter taught a summer course in Children's Literature. Assistant to Helen Heffernan of California's Department of Education, Potter was a well-known education reformer who used her office to push for a more child-centered curriculum. Stressing the important role libraries played in developing "social competence" among children, Potter (1942) believed that books had "the power to extend and deepen social sensitivity beyond first-hand contacts" as well as open "new vistas, new points of view, and new understandings" (p. 70).

Aside from Doris Gates, the department's most famous summer school instructor was Flora Belle Luddington. A 1925 graduate of the New York State Library School, Luddington was working as the head of collection development at Mills College when she taught for San José State in the early 1930s. Luddington left California in 1936, when she was appointed head librarian at Mount Holyoke College, a position she held until 1964. During her distinguished career, Luddington advocated for national and international cooperation and was an outspoken proponent of intellectual freedom during the heat of the McCarthy era. Following her election as ALA president in 1953, Luddington returned to San José State, where faculty and students hosted a reception in her honor (*Summertimes*, 1953).

Conclusion

This ambitious summer school program not only enabled the department to survive during the hardships of the Great Depression and World War II, it also firmly established San José State as a leading player in the development of school librarianship in California. SLIS faculty served as officers in the California Library Association and the California School Library Association. Dora Smith, Joyce Backus, Helen Bullock, and Flora Belle Luddington chaired important committees; others, like Margaret Girdner, Doris Gates, and Robert Gitler, published books and articles on school libraries and library science education. The department's graduates were also beginning to make an impact on the state's library community by holding positions in school, public, and county libraries, serving with their former teachers on professional association committees, and making their own contribution to the professional literature.

Backus's ambitions for her department and its faculty would begin to move forward with the end of the war and the influx of new students who had left wartime jobs. Libraries were once again hiring new graduates and, based on employer inquiries made to the school, a significant shift was occurring away from the teacher-librarian model toward hiring fully credentialed librarians to run school libraries full time. San José State itself had a brand new library building that opened in 1941, enabling its collections, facilities and professional staff to expand and improve significantly in the next decade. In 1952, MacQuarrie retired as college president. This would begin a new era in SLIS's early history.

Chapter 4

Expanding the Focus: The School Library Media Program and Other Specializations, 1945-1969

> Librarians are accepting the complexity of the twentieth century technology but it is not easy. It requires a background of information using all communication media as well as achieving a broad knowledge of academic fields. "Multi-media libraries" require "media-oriented librarians."
>
> —Jean Wichers
> SLIS Faculty
> 1966[11]

With the war's end, San José State was infused with renewed spirit and vitality that made possible many of the Department of Librarianship's long-deferred plans. After 1945, the college advanced dramatically, leaving behind its traditional teacher-training role to become a comprehensive regional university. Key to San José State's modernization was John Wahlquist, who replaced retiring president Thomas MacQuarrie in 1952. During his first year in office, President Wahlquist severed connections with the junior college and significantly enlarged San José State's undergraduate and graduate programs. At the

[11] Wichers, J. (1966, May). An approach to communimedia. *California School Libraries,* 37(4), 24.

same time, he doubled the college's teaching staff, endeavoring to recruit prestigious faculty from the nation's top universities (Walsh, 2003, p. 2-3). Student numbers increased accordingly. In the fall of 1945, the college had approximately 2,500 students. A decade later there were more than 8,500 students on campus. When Wahlquist retired in 1964, SJSU's student body reached 20,000 (Gilbert & Burdick, pp. 148, 157, 158).

San José State's postwar development coincided with a push from the ALA to raise academic standards for professional education. The Board of Education for Librarianship (BEL) sought to make the professional degree graduate-level only and eliminate outdated undergraduate options. This was accomplished in 1951 when the BEL revised its library school accreditation standards. At the same time, the ALA fully divested itself of accrediting school library programs, giving the responsibility to the newly formed American Association of Colleges for Teacher Education (AACTE). A few years later, in 1954, the AACTE created a separate accrediting body—the National Council for Accreditation of Teacher Education (NCATE)—to oversee training programs in school librarianship. From this point forward, San José State's Department of Librarianship, like other combined credential and graduate programs, was accountable to two separate accrediting agencies, as well as to the California Board of Education and its own college administration.

Embracing the new mood on campus, the Department of Librarianship entered into a period of marked growth, hiring new faculty, adding new courses, and graduating more and more students. In 1950, Joyce Backus, the Department of Librarianship founder, resigned as department chair. Thus it fell to her successor, Dora Smith, to guide the library science program's expansion and change. Smith's appointment was as a full-time department chair. This was a significant milestone in the program's history, as it meant the Department of Librarianship was now an academic unit separate from the library's administration.

Smith's first responsibility as department chair was to increase the number of graduating students to meet the surging postwar market for trained librarians, particularly in schools. "The need for school librarians is urgent," she wrote in a 1953 memo to campus administrators. Citing figures from the college's placement office showing that requests for qualified librarians had risen over 500%, Smith urged the new college president to allow her "to expand and build up a department which will be able to meet this demand more adequately" (Application for Approval of a Masters Degree Program, 1953, p. 8, SJSU Archives).

Not only were more students enrolling in San José State's library science program, they were also more diverse in their professional interests and goals. While most students still planned on working in schools, the majority sought positions as full-time librarians rather than as teacher- librarians. Other students desired to work with children in public libraries, so much so that in 1949, the department began offering a second degree option in this area.

In addition to expanding the numbers of students and classes, Smith also needed to convince San José State administrators that the department must develop a master's degree program to meet ALA's new accreditation standards. As she explained to campus officials, "The increasing demands of the modern school and its curricula require of school librarians a broader type of professional education than is possible on the undergraduate level." Graduate courses were essential, she continued, for San José State to remain competitive with other library schools. "Professional education for librarianship has been undergoing significant changes since 1948," she argued. "Since that time nearly all accredited library schools have established new graduate programs leading to the masters degree" (Application for Approval of a Masters Degree Program, 1953, pp. 1, 4, SJSU Archives).

The department's plans to develop a graduate degree advanced when, in 1951, San José State created the Division of Education, containing the Department of Librarianship and the Department of Education as equals. Now an independent academic unit, the library science department could pursue its own course. Accordingly, in October 1953, Smith submitted to the college administration an "Application for Approval of a Masters Degree in School Librarianship at San José State College." President Wahlquist approved the MA degree shortly thereafter, and the Department of Librarianship inaugurated its new MA in school librarianship in the 1954-1955 academic year.

Curriculum

The department's curriculum had been undergoing continual revision since the end of the war, so creating a new graduate-level program was not as complicated as might be expected. Courses had already been revised to reflect changing information technologies, and increasingly they focused on librarianship rather than teaching books and reading. The number of collection development courses was reduced, and in their stead several new courses were added, including Principles of Librarianship and Promoting Library Use. Other courses that had been part of the curriculum for years were renumbered so that they would now be at the graduate level. Most significant to the program's new graduate degree was the creation of two new research courses: LIBR 298 (Special Studies) and LIBR 299 (Thesis). In fact, all students in the MA program wrote a thesis for their "culminating experience."

Thus, the department's curricular innovation during the 1950s was not driven by the graduate versus undergraduate dichotomy, but instead reflected the enormous changes taking place in information technology and the increasing importance of audiovisual materials in school libraries. Initially, the library profession considered books and media as distinct—even incompatible—entities that should be administered by different personnel with different academic training. In fact, school librarians often viewed audiovisual materials as a passing fad and not of their concern.

Reflecting this prevailing paradigm, San José State's library science curriculum remained book-centered until the mid 1950s, at which point the faculty began advocating a new theory of school librarianship. In a 1955 article, "School Library Training Looks Ahead," Smith explained her department's changing views: "Since printed materials and audio-visual materials are both instruments of communication and serve as instructional devices, their use should be correlated in a single program" (p. 185). School librarians, Smith elaborated, should be equipped to handle all types of curricular materials, not just books. This emerging professional philosophy became known as the "unity of materials" approach to school libraries and school librarianship.

In 1954, the department codified this new "unity of materials" concept into a new master's degree option called "Curriculum Materials." Students in this specialization took a combination of library science and instructional technology classes relating to audiovisual collections. These courses, often taught in the Education Department, included Organization and Administration of the Curriculum Materials Center, Curriculum Building Materials, and Selection and Evaluation of Audiovisual Materials.

To keep pace with new technologies, other faculty began to incorporate audiovisual technologies into their own courses. For example, in the late 1950s, the department tapped into San José State's new television production studio to establish a closed-circuit link to several nearby high schools. Students in Leslie Janke's School Library Administration course used this early experiment in reality TV to observe the goings-on in the school libraries. In her class on School and Library Relations, Marjorie Limbocker used the TV studios to film students' storytelling efforts and their practice library instruction sessions (Janke, 1959, p. 6). "San Jose is the only librarianship training school in the United States," Leslie Janke boasted, " to utilize closed-circuit television in its observation and instruction program" (Annual Report, 1962/1963, p. 2, SLIS Archives).

To fully capitalize on curricular opportunities offered by the latest audiovisual technologies, the department secured several new faculty members savvy in emerging media. The first new hire was Leslie Janke, who joined the department in the fall of 1956. An expert in audiovisual instructional material with an MA in Curriculum Materials from Florida State University, Janke quickly added new classes to the library department's course offerings. These included Organization of Curriculum Materials, Administration of School Libraries, and even American Magazines. Janke was also instrumental in establishing the college's Instructional Technology Department. In 1959 he was appointed chair of the Department of Librarianship.

Accreditation

By 1960, San José State's Department of Librarianship had expanded sufficiently to seriously pursue ALA accreditation. Although the department had always used ALA's educational standards to shape its curricular content, its desire to apply for accreditation had been forestalled by local and institutional constraints. As discussed in chapter 3, President MacQuarrie opposed national professional accrediting bodies and refused to initiate any movement toward ALA accreditation. Even after MacQuarrie retired, the department's narrow school library focus was not in keeping with ALA's 1951 standards, which exclusively accredited general library science programs. The ALA further stipulated that a library science curriculum must contain a series of foundational classes that addressed core "professional principles and methods" which all students, regardless of specialization, were required to take (Carroll, 1970, p. 262). By contrast, San José State's three degree specializations—school libraries, public libraries, and curriculum materials—had different requirements.

Perhaps most vexing was the problem of the department's undergraduate library science degree. In 1957, the ALA ceased accrediting undergraduate library science programs, arguing that librarians needed a full liberal arts education before embarking upon professional training at the graduate level. Yet, according to the standards established by the California Board of Education, one could still qualify for the state's school librarianship credential with an undergraduate major in library science. As the only institution within the state university system authorized to teach library science courses, San José State was obliged to continue its undergraduate degree, contrary to ALA dictates. Throughout the 1950s, then, the Department of Librarianship offered both graduate and undergraduate degrees.

Fortunately, in the early 1960s, changes in California's education code made it possible for the Department of Librarianship to eliminate this accreditation roadblock. In 1961, the California Legislature passed the Licensing and Certificated Personnel Act to bolster the general education and subject expertise of California's teachers. Popularly known as the "Fisher Act," this important legislation made the teaching credential a post-baccalaureate degree, so that students had to earn an academic BA before seeking their credential. This change applied to the special credential in librarianship as well, so that now San José State's teacher-training students had to possess a subject BA before seeking library science certification. The Fisher Act went into effect in 1963; the very next year, San José State's Department of Librarianship dropped its undergraduate program so that it solely awarded fifth-year degrees.

As the department phased out its undergraduate courses (current students were given two years to finish their BAs), the entire curriculum was revamped to meet the needs of a more comprehensive, graduate-level library school. New required "core" classes were developed and specialty classes added. Initially, MA students could choose from three tracks: school librarianship, curriculum materials, and public librarianship. In 1967, a fourth specialization in college and special libraries was added, supported by new courses in these areas.

The department's expansion and renewed interest in accreditation now had the strong support of the college's administration. To be in compliance with ALA standards, the department requested in September 1967 to officially separate from the School of Education to become an independent "school" on campus. The State University's chancellor refused on the grounds that San José State already had its quota of school-level academic units. As a compromise, in January 1968, San José State Academic Vice President Hobart Burns placed the Department of Librarianship under the administrative oversight of the dean of graduate studies. This repositioning met ALA standards and moved the accreditation process one step further.

Before officially approaching the ALA to request an accreditation review, the department hired its old friend, Robert Gitler, now librarian at the University of San Francisco, to evaluate the current program. It also sought advice from eminent library science educator Bohdan Wynar, dean of the library school at the University of New York at Geneseo, regarding its curricular structure and content. Based on Gitler's and Wynar's feedback, the department revised its program one more time. The final curriculum submitted to the ALA consisted of five required "core" classes: Selection of Materials, Basic Reference Materials and Services, Technical Services, Foundations of Librarianship, and Library Management. To specialize, students took at least one course dealing with a specific type of literature (Humanities, Social Science, Science, or Children's and Young Adults) and one course focusing on a specific type of library. At the conclusion of their coursework, students had the option of writing a thesis or taking the research methods course and passing a comprehensive exam. All other courses were elective, based on a student's career interests and goals.

In September 1968, with strong support from San José State President Robert Clark, Department Chair Les Janke formally approached Lester

Asheim, director of ALA's Office of Library Education, to schedule a formal review (Janke to Asheim, 10 September 1968, ALA Archives). After some negotiation, the ALA appointed an evaluation team comprised of Marion Milczewski, director of libraries, University of Washington; Kenneth Vance, associate professor, University of Michigan Department of Library Science; and Agnes Reagan, executive secretary of ALA's Library Education Division.[12] Taking place from May 7 to May 9, the review went smoothly. The ALA rendered its final decision in June, and in July 1969 the official letter from the Office for Library Education finally arrived. Signed by Agnes Reagan, Assistant Director for Accreditation, the announcement read:

> It is a pleasure to send you official notice that the Committee on Accreditation of the American Library Association at its meeting June 23, 1969 voted to accredit the program leading to the degree of Master of Arts in Librarianship offered by the Department of Librarianship of San Jose State College, under the standards for Accreditation adopted by the ALA Council, July 13, 1951. The accreditation is retroactive to cover the academic year preceding the year in which the accreditation visit was made. (Reagan to Janke, 7 July 1969, ALA Archives)

Faculty

The Department of Librarianship's expansion in the 1950s and its final push to achieve ALA accreditation the following decade required a major reorientation in how faculty were appointed and used. The department reduced its ties with the college library staff so that by the mid-1960s instructors were recruited nationwide and selected for their

[12] Originally, Margaret Monroe, chair of the University of Wisconsin Library School, was appointed to the team. But in late April she suffered a knee injury and had to be replaced by Dr. Reagan.

subject expertise and academic credentials rather than drafted from the on-campus library pool. And while most faculty continued to have a background in school libraries, their research and teaching interests were much broader.

During the 1940s and 1950s, the department's teaching and administration fell to longtime library staffers Dora Smith and Jeannette Vander Ploeg. By the early 1950s, Smith and Vander Ploeg had full-time faculty appointments, assisted by Marjorie Martin Limbocker, who had joined San José State's library in 1945. Interestingly, Limbocker, whose MLS was from the University of Michigan, was one of the early students in San José State's Curriculum Materials specialization, completing her second master's in 1956. Thereafter, she taught many of the department's school library media classes until she retired in 1966. Smith,Vander Ploeg, and Limbocker nurtured the department during this transitional period, teaching an endless stream of classes, advising student groups, hosting social and professional events, and planning the annual summer sessions. They were professionally active and played leading roles in California's school library community. When Smith and Vander Ploeg both retired in 1958, it was truly the end of an era.

While Smith, Vander Ploeg, and Limbocker constituted the Department of Librarianship's regular faculty in the 1950s, other San José State librarians taught courses in their areas of specialization. Robert Lauritzen, for example, started working for the library immediately after earning his MLS from Berkeley in 1952. A reference librarian and bibliographer, he taught various courses, most notably in the area of collection development. Jerome Munday and Milton Loventhal also taught for the department during their time with the college library. With an MLS from UC Berkeley, Munday spent his entire career at San José State, working in the library from 1955-1988. Loventhal, another UC Berkeley alum, joined San José State's library faculty in 1959. During his long career at the university (he retired in 1992 to pursue playwriting), Loventhal published numerous bibliographies as well as taught regularly in the Department of Librarianship.

Perhaps most interesting among these in-house instructors was Ruth Marie Baldwin, whose career at San José State lasted from 1946 to 1949. Originally from South Carolina, Baldwin earned her BS and MLS from University of Illinois. While employed as a reference librarian at San José State, she taught courses in children's literature and bibliographic instruction, then called "Library Use." After leaving San José State in 1949, Baldwin returned to the University of Illinois to earn a PhD whereupon she joined the faculty at Louisiana State University. An avid children's book collector, Baldwin donated over 35,000 books to the University of Florida, Gainesville, in 1977. After her death in 1990, the ALA created the Louise Seaman Betchel Fellowship in her honor to fund scholarly research in the Baldwin children's book collection at the University of Florida.

In addition to taking advantage of on-campus specialists, the department also tapped some of its own graduates to teach courses during the 1950s and 1960s. As the only college in the state offering an MA in curriculum materials, the department had to cultivate individuals with this rare expertise. Janice Lieberman, for example, earned both her school library credential and an MA in curriculum materials from San José State. After spending several years as a cataloger at Stanford University's Art Museum, she returned to San José State to teach cataloging and school libraries courses. Mildred Vick Chatton was another alum who devoted her career to teaching for the department. A Virginia native, Chatton earned a BA in library science from the University of North Carolina, before obtaining a school library credential and an MA in curriculum materials from San José State. Graduating in 1966, she began teaching school media courses for the department and in 1967 was elected president of the California School Library Association.

Another curriculum materials alum was Jean Wichers, who taught for the department until her sudden death in 1983. A strong advocate for the "unity of materials" approach to school libraries, Wichers wrote extensively on the topic, arguing that today's multimedia school libraries needed "media-oriented librarians" (Wichers, 1966, p. 24). Her influence in the field was not only felt in the classroom but also in her work as an officer in the American Association of School Librarians, California Library Association, and the California School Library Association, as well as during her stint as *School Libraries* editor.

With the opportunity to bring in several new full-time faculty members in 1958, Department Chair Les Janke was in a position to reinvent the department along more contemporary lines. Gone were the days when the library and library science personnel were interchangeable. Professional and state accrediting bodies required that library departments have a full-time faculty with academic credentials equivalent to other departments on campus.

When Irene Norell and Shirley Hopkinson joined the department in 1959, a new era in the library school's history was launched. Hopkinson was one of the first faculty members with a doctorate, having earned her EdD in audiovisual education from the University of Oklahoma in 1957. Originally from Boone, Iowa, Hopkinson had taught high school before deciding to become a librarian and earning an MLS at UC Berkeley. She worked as a librarian at both Modesto and Chaffey Junior Colleges before joining the faculty at San José State. During her long career (she retired in 1992) Hopkinson taught a variety of classes ranging from research methods to serials, though increasingly her courses focused on cataloging and technical services. She also published extensively, including seven books on cataloging and instructional materials. When she retired in 1992, students presented her with a music box that played "Unforgettable."

Although Irene Norell did not have a doctorate (she had an MA in history from San José State and her library science degree was from the University of Minnesota), she was the first faculty hired with a teaching specialization in something other than school libraries. Having worked professionally in public libraries in Minnesota and North Dakota, Norell taught many of the department's non-school related courses. In the 1970s, she became very interested in contemporary social issues and developed innovative, socially conscious courses such as Library Outreach to the Unserved.

Among the more erudite of the new instructors was Willard O. Mishoff, who began teaching classes in reference and bibliography in 1962. With professional degrees from the University of Michigan and the University of Chicago, and a PhD in history from the University of Iowa, Mishoff had a distinguished professional library career as an academic and research librarian before coming to San José State. He spent 15 years as the library specialist in the U.S. Office of Education

(1943-1958) and was a faculty member in the library science program at Mississippi State College for Women before moving to California.[13]

In the build-up to accreditation the department was able to expand its full-time faculty significantly. In fact, in 1967 and 1968 three new instructors were hired: James Cabeceiras, Donald Witting, and William Bliss Wood. Although only Cabeceiras had a doctorate, each brought an academic expertise that was vital to the department's curricular development. With a PhD in instructional technology from Syracuse University (1967), Cabeceiras not only developed courses in multimedia, he also counseled other faculty in how to incorporate information science content into their courses as well. Donald Wittig was a renaissance man, with degrees in electrical engineering, theology, music, and library science. An artist as well, Wittig contributed cartoons to ALA's *American Libraries.* Wittig helped the department develop its new specialization in academic libraries, focusing his teaching on research methods, college library service, and literature of the sciences. William Wood had taught at the University of British Columbia before coming to San José State in 1967. Wood, like Wittig, was vital to the department's new course offerings in academic and special libraries, teaching courses in reference services, government documents, and literature of the humanities.

Between 1945 and 1969, the library science faculty was transformed. After the war and throughout much of the 1950s the department continued to hire San José State librarians and alumni to teach its courses. Most had background and expertise in teaching and school libraries, as was appropriate given the program's curricular focus. By the end of the 1960s, however, the department had dramatically changed. Its new faculty had been recruited nationwide and their areas of expertise were much broader. In 1958, no faculty member had a PhD. In 1968, nine of the instructors had doctorates. Although the department still ranked among the lowest on campus in terms of faculty PhDs, to the ALA it showed marked improvement, especially given the limited number of library science doctorates awarded each

[13] The Mishoff collection in San José State's University Archives and Special Collections Department contains numerous books and pamphlets Mishoff acquired during his time working for the federal government.

year (Graduate Program Statistics, 1968, p. 11, SJSU Archives). More to the point, these changes in faculty were sufficient to meet ALA's looming accreditation standards.

Students

Changing student demographics attest to the remarkable expansion of San José State's library science program in the 1950s and 1960s. Between 1946 and 1952, the program averaged eight students, graduating four or five per year. Almost all came from California (94%), with 71% residing in nearby towns and 57% still living at home (Leigh, 1952, p. 72). San José State's professional degree was a bargain compared to other library schools in the state: San José State students paid $49.80 annual tuition, whereas a year's fees at UC Berkeley were $88.20 and a whopping $465.20 at the University of Southern California (Leigh, 1952, p. 78). It must be remembered, however, that UC Berkeley and University of Southern California were graduate-level library schools while San José State was still an undergraduate program at this time. This situation was about to change.

In the fall of 1953, the department started offering "extended day" and evening classes, and student numbers began to rise. Forty students were enrolled in library science courses in the 1952/1953 academic year. When San José State began its master's program in the fall of 1954, its students more than doubled, with 101 now in the program (Annual Report, 1952-1957, p. 1, SJSU Archives). The department grew steadily thereafter, and when it went up for accreditation in the spring of 1969, more than 230 students were seeking their MA or special credential, making librarianship the second largest graduate program on campus.[14]

Particularly striking about these students is that the majority were part-time, taking courses in the late afternoon and evening. For example, in 1954/1955, the first year that the MA in school librarianship was offered, there were 23 full-time students and 70 part-time ones. Every year thereafter, part-time students outnumbered full-time ones, though

[14] The Department of Education's teaching credential program had more than 400 students in 1969.

never again in quite such striking numbers. In the spring of 1969, 56% of the student body was attending class part-time (155 part-time students versus 119 full-time students).

These new students also had a much broader range of professional aspirations than those in previous decades. Until 1949, all students concentrated on the school library specialization, despite the department's claim that its courses also prepared students for work with children in public libraries. Even after the public library work with children specialization was added in 1949, San José State remained, in essence, a training program for school librarians and, after 1955, curriculum materials specialists.

The part-time program combined with more classes and faculty expert in other professional specializations broadened the program's appeal. Between 1946 and 1951, 71% of its graduates reported working in school libraries. By 1969, students were more evenly distributed between school library and non-school library tracks.

- 98 credentials
- 27 MA degrees in school libraries
- 65 MA degrees in public libraries
- 10 MA degrees in college/special libraries
- 2 MS degrees in curriculum materials

While the department's annual reports provide intriguing statistical data regarding the department's changing student body, they include no information regarding gender or ethnic background until the 1970s. As a result, personal details about San José State students in the 1950s and 1960s are hard to find. One of the earliest discussions of "diversity" can be found in Robert Leigh's 1952 study of California library schools. In his report, Leigh noted that although the GI Bill encouraged a large number of men to enroll in UC Berkeley's library science program after the war, it did not have the same impact at San José State. Whereas in 1951/1952 males accounted for 28% of UC Berkeley's library science students, males represented less than 10% at San José State (Leigh, 1952, pp. 67, 69). This makes sense given the nature of the school library workforce. According to Leigh, 97% of librarians in public elementary schools and 95% of librarians in high schools were women

(p. 44). San José State's male/female ratio did improve modestly as the program diversified and more males joined the faculty. Indeed, when Les Janke became the advisor for the library science student association in 1958, 4 of the 14 members were men. In 1969, males accounted for 18% of the student body.

As for ethnic background, data does not exist. Judging from names and photographs appearing in college yearbooks and the *Spartan Daily*, the department's students continued to be overwhelmingly white and female. The program graduated its first minority student in 1953—Japanese American Marie Sakaguchi. Born in San José in 1932, Sakaguchi's family had spent the war years incarcerated at Heart Mountain Relocation Center, Wyoming, and returned to California after the war. The color barrier having been broken, other ethnic women—though admittedly not many—entered the program: Shirley Ligon (African American) in 1954; June Michiko Chikasuye (Japanese American) and Marie Doi (Japanese American) in 1955; and Kyoko Inoue, a student from Japan, in 1958. The first nonwhite male student appears to have been Bernard Leong (Chinese American) of the class of 1958.

We know about these ethnic students because they were pictured in the *La Torre* yearbook among the Alpha Beta Alpha (ABA) Fraternity, a national association for library science students that was formed in 1952 and supplanted the Bibliophiles in the mid 1950s (*La Torre*, 1958, p. 92). Gone with the Bibliophiles were the teas, picnics, and social events. In the 1950s and 1960s, the student culture took on a more professional tone, and the ABA focused its activities around professional meetings, "wholesome recreation," and recruiting new students into the field (*La Torre*, 1958, p. 92). The ABA was also engaged in various social causes. For example, in 1955, the student group sponsored two ambitious programs: the "Pencils Please" project to send pencils to Korean children and a book drive for an orphanage in Burma (*La Torre*, 1955, n.p.). In 1957 and 1958, the ABA collected books for Native American children in New Mexico and Alaska (*La Torre*, 1957, n.p.).

Alpha Beta Alpha's members were typical of the library department's students who went on to have full and rewarding careers. For example, 1955 president Trudy Jansens spent her career working at San José

Public Library. Dolores Vinal, who was involved in the 1954 group, became a librarian at Redwood City's McKinley School. Alverda Orlando, a 1954-1955 ABA member, spent her career at the Santa Cruz Public Library, where she became well known as a local historian and author.

The most noteworthy student to graduate from San José State's library science department during this period was Ethel Crockett, who served as California State Librarian from 1972 to 1980. Crockett—a Vassar College alumna—worked as a children's librarian in New York, before moving to California to earn her library science degree at San José State. Crockett's first position after receiving her MLS in 1962 was as a reference librarian at San José City College. She then became director of library services at San Francisco City College before her 1972 appointment as California State Librarian. Crockett's support and advocacy of San José State's library science program would become very important in the 1970s.

Summer School

Summer school was a perfect venue to promote the department's modern multimedia focus and continue San José State's preeminence in the training of school library media specialists. Throughout the 1950s, summer session enrollments outpaced those in regular session, as employed teacher-librarians used the summer months to obtain their school librarianship credentials. In 1949, Joyce Backus estimated that 35 students in the summer program were seeking the special credential (*Summertimes,* 16 August 1949). More than a decade later, Les Janke reported to the university that 158 students were taking summer school courses, the highest enrollment ever. The summer students' education goals were still much the same. As Janke wrote in 1962, they were "in-service librarians returning to complete work on credentials or Master's degrees" (Annual Report, 1961/1962, p.2, SLIS Archives).

San José State continued its tradition of hiring visiting instructors to teach summer courses, adding depth and variety to the department's curricular offerings. Some of the more interesting of these adjuncts were:

- Geraldine Ferring, San Francisco Bureau of Texts and Libraries
- Charlotte Davis, Coordinator of Library Services for the Santa Barbara County School District (1959)
- Dr. Paulina O'Melia, Director of Libraries for the Long Island, New York Schools (1961)
- Dr. Earl Strohbehn, U.S. Department of Secondary Education (1961)
- Rachael DeAngelo, Professor, Department of Library Science, Drexel Institute (1965)
- Dr. John Farley, Chair, Department of Library Science, Queens College, CUNY (1967)

However, once the department began its part-time evening program the overall importance of summer sessions waned. Although many teacher-librarians continued to take advantage of summer sessions to earn their credentials, more and more students were also enrolled in courses during the academic year, so that by the mid-1960s, enrollment ratios had reversed. Now there were twice as many students in the regular academic program as there were in summer school classes. Eventually, summer school ceased to be the department's major source of students and income and became more regularized as a third academic semester.

With summer school becoming less important, the department began experimenting with new ventures, using San José State resources and facilities to offer week-long workshops and institutes. The first summer institute, called "Patterns for Progress," was put on by Dora Smith in June 1957. "A workshop has been a dream of mine ever since coming to San José," Smith wrote to former colleague Robert Gitler, who was then ALA's executive secretary. "It's thrilling to see it become a reality and under Mrs. Douglas!" (Smith to Gitler, 11 February 1957, ALA Archives). Mrs. Douglas was Mary Peacock Douglas, a nationally recognized expert in school libraries who had chaired the ALA committee that developed the first national standards for school libraries in 1945. Recipient of ALA's prestigious Grolier Award in 1958, Douglas's institute was open to "all school librarians, teacher-librarians, and persons interested in curriculum center development," and focused on the latest methods of school library programming. As part of the workshop, an evening reception was held to honor two esteemed guests: Lucille Fargo and Carolyn Mott Kean. Kean was a San José State alum who, in the 1940s, published several important school library textbooks. Fargo, who was retired and living in Berkeley, was the nation's foremost authority on school libraries during the 1920s and 1930s, authoring the first major studies on the topic, most notably *The Library in the School* (1930) and *The Program for Elementary School Library Service* (1930). Smith's inaugural summer workshop was a smashing success, attracting over 250 participants from throughout the country.

The following summer Smith organized a series of seminars given, as she described it, by "outstanding figures in the field of librarianship" (Annual Report, 1958/1959, p. 2, SLIS Archives). Capitalizing on ALA's annual conference taking place in San Francisco, Smith was able to attract a number of attendees to San José State's campus. These included Robert Gitler, who spoke on his experiences in Japan, and eminent library science educator and author Louis Shores, who discussed current developments in the field of curriculum materials. Other notable speakers were Mary K. Eakin, former librarian at the University of Chicago's Center for Children's Books, and Ruth Ersted, Minnesota State Supervisor of School Libraries and past president of the American Association of School Librarians.

In 1960, Mary Peacock returned to San José State to lead another week-long workshop titled "Books and Beyond." Two-hundred and twenty-five teachers and administrators attended to learn more about current trends in school library media centers. The department published the proceedings of the class sessions, selling over 500 copies. A copy of *Books and Beyond: A Workshop in Curriculum Enrichment*, by Mary Peacock Douglas, is still available in San José State University's Dr. Martin Luther King, Jr. Library.

Later in the 1960s, the department successfully competed for federal grants to fund additional institutes. For example, in 1964, the Department of Education (which at the time included the Departments of Librarianship and Instructional Technology) was awarded a National Defense Education Act grant to fund a month-long "Educational

Media Specialists' Institute." Geared toward classroom teachers responsible for coordinating their school's media services, the institute covered all aspects of curriculum materials and their use, with a special focus on the use of television in modern instructional programs. The department sponsored another grant-funded institute in August 1969. Under the direction of Professor Jean Wichers, this four-week program dealt with communication skills needed to provide library services to children in "culturally different communities." Innovative for its time, the workshop was directed at librarians working in schools and public libraries serving bilingual students. Its curriculum dealt with how traditional children's programming might be adapted for new population groups.

The department's openness to various modes of delivering professional and continuing education via summer courses and institutes was evident in another area of experimental education during this time. As the only state college in Northern California authorized by the California Department of Education to offer courses leading to the school librarianship credential, it was incumbent upon San José State to make the degree program as widely available as possible. And although San José State's program was still not accredited by the ALA, since its courses were authorized by the state, its graduates had no difficulty finding jobs. Indeed, Department Chair Les Janke declared in his 1962/1963 annual report that "all graduates since 1959 have been placed" (p.4).

To capitalize on its unique niche in library science education, the Department of Librarianship began experimenting with off-site courses in 1957. The first class, Book Selection for School Libraries, was taught in Santa Cruz. A seeming success, the department taught two off-site courses the following semester, one in Santa Cruz and another in Palo Alto, attracting 20 and 38 students, respectively. Other off-site classes were added in Fresno, Monterey, and Pleasant Hill in 1960; and in 1962, the department added Bakersfield as well. The Department of Librarianship would continue to offer courses at various locations over the next decade as it sought to meet the state's demand for professionally educated librarians. This would culminate in 1989 when San José State opened a full off-site library science program at its sister campus, California State University, Fullerton.

Conclusion

The two decades that followed the Second World War witnessed vast changes in San José State's Department of Librarianship. The program evolved from an undergraduate degree to a master's level program and broadened its original school library emphasis to offer specializations in public, academic, and special librarianship as well. The department's faculty expanded and improved, and for the first time, the department was able to recruit full-time faculty with advanced research degrees. The department continued its tradition of employing prominent part-time and visiting faculty which added depth and excitement to the school's regular programming. San José State's student numbers increased dramatically, a consequence of both the implementation of a master's degree program and the experimentation with flexible scheduling, which enabled students to attend classes part time, in the evenings, and even at sites other than San José State.

By 1969 the Department of Librarianship was not only the largest master's degree program on campus, it also graduated more librarians than any other school in the state. Now a general, graduate-level program, it was finally accorded full ALA accreditation in June 1969. In a report that the Committee on Accreditation sent to the department regarding its accreditation findings, the review team made several recommendations that would shape the library school's development in the coming decade. Of most significance was the following observation:

> It is the feeling of the visiting team that without de-emphasizing the program to prepare librarians for work with children in school and public libraries, the Department should move ahead as rapidly as possible to develop strong specializations in academic and special librarianship and in other aspects of public library work. The team wishes to stress also that the Department's degree program should be of first importance with preparation for the school library credential a secondary concern of the school. Being the kind of college that it is, San Jose has a responsibility to

> offer work for the credential, but the major focus of the Department should be on the Master's program. (COA Report, [1969], p.17, SLIS Archives)

The ALA would be monitoring San José's progress toward these ends as the program and its university entered the turbulent 1970s.

Chapter 5

Adding Information Science: San José State's MLIS Degree, 1969-1989

> Focusing on the solutions possible to us in library education today is one of the most challenging and exciting opportunities we can have. Hearing practitioners talk about the irrelevance of library school curriculum, I agree with some of their complaints, but I want to go on and develop a model for change, not just air my dissatisfactions. We are all in this together.
>
> —Elizabeth Rosen
> SLIS Faculty
> 1987[15]

The gale forces driving the Department of Librarianship during the 1970s and 1980s can be best described as a perfect storm. A confluence of pressure from the ALA, San José State administrators, politically active students, and fast-paced technological change pulled the program in many, sometimes conflicting, directions. Although the ALA had accredited the department in 1969, its Committee on Accreditation (COA) had continuing concerns that San José State's curriculum privileged the school library media program to the detriment of

[15] Rosen, E. M. (1987, winter). Educators and practitioners: A cooperative pattern of curriculum review. *Top of the News, 43,* 185.

other specializations. In a series of annual reviews, the ALA urged the department to hire new faculty to teach classes in academic and special libraries and to add more information science coursework. The ALA also criticized the department's limited access to computers and the latest library software.

At the same time that the ALA was encouraging the department to expand its faculty, courses, and technological infrastructure, San José State University (SJSU)[16] was grappling with an unexpected downturn in students. In fact, declining student enrollments in both the 1974 and 1975 academic years obliged the university to return to the state previously allocated funds (Gilbert & Burdick, 1980, p. 206). This financial crunch forced the university to limit new faculty hiring and seek innovative ways for academic units to share resources and expertise. As Department Chair Les Janke explained to ALA's Committee on Accreditation, there was pressure from SJSU and California State University (CSU) administrators to use existing faculty and resources to develop new programs. Duplication and proliferation of courses were "rigorously discouraged" (Appeal, 1975, p. 26, SLIS Archives). So, at the very time that ALA's officials demanded that SJSU's library science program expand, the university required cutbacks. As a result, the Department of Librarianship was unable to meet certain ALA conditions, and in the summer of 1975 its accreditation was not renewed.[17]

The department devoted the next few years to getting accreditation reinstated, which happened in January 1979. Ironically, SJSU's struggle with the ALA over accreditation put the department in the position of defending its existing program rather than allowing it to evolve naturally in response to the revolutionary social and technological changes of the late 1960s and 1970s. However, once accreditation was finally and permanently restored, the Department of Librarianship—now the Division of Library Science—reinvented itself, developing an institutional identity and culture that would transform it into the world's largest library science program.

---

[16] San José State College was renamed San José State University in 1974.

[17] The library science programs at the University of Oklahoma and the University of Rhode Island also lost accreditation at this time.

Curriculum

Despite discouraging fiscal circumstances during much of the 1970s, Department Chair Janke did his best to implement many of the changes the ALA had recommended in its original 1969 accreditation report. Academic Vice President Hobart Burns supported the department's efforts and located funds to hire new faculty and improve the library's professional and technological resources. Burns also approached the CSU Chancellor's Office about raising the department to division status and reclassifying its chair as dean. Because of the state university's reluctance to make administrative change during this period of financial crisis, the department would not become the Division of Library Science until 1977.

Having addressed the key administrative issues raised in ALA's accreditation report, the library science department attacked its curriculum on several fronts. The faculty reviewed its core courses and made a concerted effort to ensure that their content was appropriate for and relevant to all library specializations and not just school libraries. In keeping with the university's policy to use existing resources and personnel, the Department of Librarianship forged alliances with other units on campus to increase its computer-related courses. In 1970-1971, the department developed a joint program with the Department of Instructional Technology, allowing school library students to choose from a broader array of media courses (Accreditation Review, 1970-1971, p. 47, SLIS Archives). In the fall of 1974, the department helped establish an interdisciplinary master's degree program in Computer and Information Science (CIS) so that library science students could earn an MS in Library Information Systems (Self-Study Report, 1974, p. 41-42, SLIS Archives).

Despite these efforts to expand and update courses, when the department came up for accreditation review in 1975 its overall curriculum still looked much like it had in 1969. Of 23 classes listed under the Department of Librarianship in the *College Bulletin*, more than half were taught in the Education Department, despite the fact that 80% of the students in the program were now pursuing the MLS degree (138 MLS vs. 39 credential). Moreover, the curriculum was still structured around the process of building different types of subject collections rather than taking a broader, more theoretical approach to professional education. For example, eight different classes were devoted to types of literature (e.g., literature of the humanities, children's literature, government documents, American magazines, etc.), while only two dealt with professional foundations. There were also only two technical services courses and two courses relating to information science. In the department's defense this official list of library science courses did not reflect fully the educational opportunities available to library science students in the mid-1970s. As Janke tried to make clear in his 1974 accreditation report: "It has long been the philosophy of the Department not to duplicate courses offered in other departments on the campus" (p. 41). So in addition to 23 library science courses, students could choose from 13 educational technology courses and 7 classes in what was then called "cybernetic systems," now known as computer and information science. Students were also encouraged to take classes in other disciplines such as English and social science.

The ALA, however, was not satisfied with the department's interdisciplinary approach. And in its accreditation assessment the COA concluded that SJSU's curriculum failed to meet the department's mission to prepare students for work in all types of libraries. In July 1975, the department got word that its accreditation had not been renewed.

The university administration, the alumni, and the professional community rushed to the program's defense, sending letters expressing shock and disbelief at ALA's actions. SJSU's President John Bunzel immediately contacted ALA Executive Director Robert Wedgeworth to request a hearing on the matter. "We are appealing the decision of the Committee on Accreditation on a number of grounds," Bunzel wrote. The president claimed that ALA's visiting team had made significant procedural errors "which resulted in either an incomplete or a distorted perception of the Librarianship program at San José State University." He also cited evidence that the 1972 ALA Accreditation Standards were not consistently or fairly applied to San José's program and that other library science programs with comparable records had been accredited whereas San José State had not (Bunzel to Wedgeworth, 10 September 1975, SLIS Archives). The president concluded by describing the ill-effects that COA's decision was already having on SJSU's program:

> We are deeply concerned with the implications for our Librarianship program and for its numerous alumni (many in responsible library positions) of the decision not to continue the accredited status of the program. The decision of the Committee on Accreditation not to reaccredit the program has already caused a certain amount of damage to the reputation of the program, whatever the eventual outcome of the appeal may be.

The department received many letters in support of the appeal. State Librarian and SJSU alum Ethel Crockett wrote that the accreditation news "came as a shock," and she expressed her "somewhat jaundiced view of the whole procedure" (Crockett to Wichers, 13 August 1975, SLIS Archives). The head of the Los Angeles County Public Library System, Carol Moss (class of 1960), was similarly "shocked" and "dismayed" at ALA's decision. Also an SLIS alum, Moss promised to "do anything else I can to assist you in appealing this most unfortunate decision" (Moss to Wichers, 21 August 1975, SLIS Archives). Former faculty member, Robert Gitler, voiced his concern as well:

> Knowing something of the School's work and its graduates over the years, and as a former library school educator and director as well as a very concerned Secretary for the Committee on Accreditation for more than four years at ALA Headquarters, I find it difficult to reconcile three factors—the School's demonstrated excellence over the years, the stature, understanding and long experience of the Visiting Team's chairman, and the resultant report. I honestly hope there will be a reconsideration at the earliest possible date to the credit and for the benefit of the stature of all concerned. (Gitler to Wichers, 13 August 1975, SLIS Archives)

Letters even appeared in ALA's periodical, *American Libraries*:

> As ALA members and as 1970 graduates of San Jose State University's Librarianship Department, we feel compelled to respond to the statement on the accreditation of SJSU's librarianship program. . . . With regard to the fact that only procedural matters are being considered in the accreditation appeal, we believe it is essential that ALA members be aware of two substantive considerations:
>
> 1) We know of no graduates of the SJSU program who are unable to perform successfully as professional librarians. And as librarian-supervisors, we have known graduates of ALA-accredited programs who can not.
> 2) The excellence in professional attitude, demeanor, and performance of the professors of SJSU's Librarianship Department is unequaled in professional circles and is unfailingly reflected in the quality of service and ideals of the program's graduates. We feel it may truly be said that SJSU's librarianship program is the finest anywhere. ("San Jose State Program," 1977, p. 14)

San José State's appeal rested on its belief that the COA committee had not followed official policy when conducting their site review. The library science department claimed that the accreditation team had not spent the requisite amount of time in San José during its official visit nor did the team members interview, as accreditation rules required, a sufficient number of faculty, students, alumni, and employers to ascertain the true quality of SJSU's program. The department also felt that the accrediting body had misunderstood or misinterpreted the data submitted in its accreditation report, particularly in regards to the number and types of courses students could take. Within the voluminous documentation submitted to the ALA in support of its appeal, the Department of Librarianship provided evidence that in the areas found to be subpar at SJSU, other accredited programs had weaker performance records.

A select committee appointed by ALA's Executive Board considered SJSU's arguments and supporting evidence. Rendering its decision on July 18, 1976, the committee affirmed ALA's initial decision to withdraw its accreditation of SJSU's library science program (Statement Concerning the Accreditation Appeal, 1976, p. 696-697).

In the long run, SJSU's temporary loss of accreditation benefited as well as hurt the program, since to get the library science department reaccredited, the university had to quickly approve and implement required changes. As future SLIS director James Healey (1980) observed, "One suspects that, thanks largely to alumni and professional support, the administration recognized—perhaps for the first time—how important a service their [library] school was providing. For a state-supported university, this is a major consideration" (p. 154).

The university's first action was to hire Lester Asheim, eminent LIS educator and former director of ALA's Office of Education, to evaluate its library science program and recommend improvements. In his report to the university president, Asheim stated that the program's core curriculum should take a "broader and more general approach" to professional education and pay greater attention to the theories and principles of professional practice. "In defining the content of the core," Asheim advised, "the emphasis should at least be as much on the 'why' of library services as on the 'how-to.'" Asheim reiterated ALA's criticism that only the school library media credential had sufficient coursework to be legitimately called a specialization. Therefore, he recommended that the department drop the thesis and reduce the number of required courses and in their place add new courses supporting the non-school library specializations. Finally, Asheim suggested that the degree name be changed from a master of arts (MA) to a master of library science (MLS), making it consistent with other professional programs on campus (e.g., Master of Business Administration and Master of Social Work) (Asheim, 1977, SLIS Archives).

With the administration's backing, the library science department acted quickly to implement Asheim's recommendations. Existing course descriptions were rewritten to bring their content in line with developing professional theories and topics. New courses such as Online Cataloging and Library Systems Design were added. Other courses—including Online Reference Service, Indexing and Abstracting, and

Information and Referral Services—were in the planning stages and would become part of the curriculum over the next few years. In 1977 the CSU Chancellor's Office agreed to raise the department to division status and authorized renaming the degree "Master of Library Science."[18]

This fast work by the department, the university, and the chancellor's office made it possible for SJSU to reapply for accreditation in 1977. Once again the department submitted to the ALA the required reports and documentation and in October 1978 hosted another accrediting team's site visit. But this time the outcome was very different. In January 1979, the ALA announced that SJSU's library science program had been reaccredited.

Preoccupied with getting, losing, and then regaining ALA accreditation, it would seem that the social and political movements of the 1960s and 1970s had passed the department by. Yet the pervasive and transformative activism both on campus and in the library profession left a lasting mark on SJSU's conception of and approach to professional education. There was a significant liberalization of program requirements to allow students to develop their own degree plans, compared to the rigid scheduling and unbending requirements that characterized the program in the 1950s and prior. Students were encouraged to get involved with campus activities and given internship credit for participating in various social programs and causes. The department even added a new course, Library Communications Seminar (LIBR 296), which faculty used to give students credit for engaging in community work.

In the 1980s, the department's interest in social causes was overshadowed by the imperatives of the computer revolution. Janke, the long-time department chair, retired in 1981. So this challenge fell initially to Guy A. Marco,[19] who served as department chair from 1981 to 1983, and then permanently in 1985 to James Healey who

---

[18] For consistency and ease of comprehension, the Division of Library and Information Science will continue to be referred to as the "department" for the remainder of this chapter.

[19] Guy Marco had served on the accreditation team that visited and reported on the program in October 1978.

would move the program in exciting new directions.[20] Both Marco and Healey marked a new orientation within the department. For one thing, both had PhDs, signifying the increasing importance of theory and research in library science education. Moreover, neither had a background in school libraries. Marco had been a research consultant and head of the Reference and Bibliography Department at the Library of Congress, while Healey worked in public libraries before becoming an LIS professor. Prior to his 1985 appointment at SJSU, Healey was director of the School of Library and Information Science at the University of Oklahoma.

With fresh leadership and several newly hired faculty members, the department completely overhauled its curriculum in the mid-1980s. In its accreditation reviews, the ALA had more than once cautioned the department that its curriculum seemed more an aggregate of courses than a unified professional education. With this stricture in mind, the faculty created a new combination of courses designed to teach students professional knowledge and skills "in a setting-free context" (Self-Study, 1985, p. 67, SLIS Archives). The motive behind this new approach was, in part, pragmatic. As faculty member Elizabeth Rosen explained in 1987, "Here in California, the results of Proposition 13 and the recessions of the last decades have fostered great bitterness among institutions vying for financial survival" (p. 185). Students thus needed a broad theoretical training to have multiple options and maximum maneuverability when they entered the tight job market.

The faculty's second objective in revising the curriculum was to create courses that were, to quote Healey (1988), "intimately intertwined with contemporary information technology" (p.18). To this end, the department secured grants from regional professional associations, the university, and the H.W. Wilson Foundation to build a microcomputer lab with the latest computers and software. Healey estimated that 65% of the courses made use of the new lab (p. 23).

Fully in place by 1988, the new curriculum nearly doubled in size, growing from 27 classes in 1982 to almost 50 classes in 1988. Students were now required to take 42 rather than 36 units. This included five core classes that students completed at the outset of their program:

[20] Professor Robert Wagers served as interim director between Marco's and Healey's administrations.

Information and Society (LIBR 200), Reference and Information Services (LIBR 201), Organization of Information (LIBR 202), Microcomputers in Libraries (LIBR 203), and Management of Library and Information Centers (LIBR 204). Students were free to choose their remaining nine courses, in consultation with their advisor. Upon completion of the coursework, students could either write a thesis or pass a four-hour comprehensive written exam.

Although there were no official curricular tracks, classes fell into five distinctive areas of specialization: Reference and Information Services, Information Science and Technology, Management and Administration, Children's and Youth Services, and Information Organization and Description. There were also numerous courses designed specifically for the region's information industry, such as Information Brokering (LIBR 234), Competitive Online Information Systems (LIBR 245), Marketing of Information Products and Services (LIBR 283), as well as online searching and management classes. The curriculum in reference services expanded most significantly, with 13 different classes now devoted to bibliography in various fields (e.g., business and economics, engineering and computer science, law, language and literature, life sciences, etc.).

Not surprisingly, information technology and systems also predominated in new course development. In May 1979, the department decided to eliminate the Library Systems option in the Computer and Information Science program. Because of the heavy emphasis on math and computer hardware, this interdisciplinary specialization was not attracting library science students. The department thus developed its own information technology courses, adding new classes such as Advanced Microcomputer Applications, Automated Library Systems, Database Management, Database Retrieval, and Computerized Online Information Systems.

Between 1969 and 1988, San José State's library science curriculum thus made a marked transition from being primarily a school library media program to a comprehensive library and information science program. Now the Division of Library and Information Science, the program gradually ended its cooperative arrangements with other departments and assumed complete responsibility for the professional coursework offered. The curriculum was greatly influenced by revolutionary changes in technology occurring during this time, and increasingly, the department considered the regional information industry as a prime employer of its graduates. In 1985, the Division officially changed its degree name to a Master of Library and Information Science, a fitting appellation for the program's new identity.

Faculty

Despite the department's plan to offer specializations in academic, special, and public libraries, the majority of faculty hired in the 1960s continued to have a school library background. This meant that much of the coursework in public, special, and academic libraries fell to part-time instructors. With the program's accreditation at risk, broadening the faculty's range of teaching and research specializations became critical. Asheim had stressed this point in his program review: "The need for an additional faculty member is crucial," he wrote to university Vice President Burns. "I cannot say that the addition of one more faculty member would insure accreditation, but I think it highly likely that without such additional faculty strength it would be difficult for the Department to meet several of the requirements of the accreditation standards" (Asheim to Burns, 11 January 1977, SLIS Archives)

The department's first priority was to recruit faculty expert in computer and information science. Two individuals can be credited with the pioneering work required to introduce new technologies into the library science program: James Dolby and Martha West. Dolby had taught for San José State's Mathematics Department since 1966 and was an early expert in what was then called "documentation," a field now known as "information retrieval." A leading authority on human-computer interaction who published extensively on topics relating to the development and use of online library catalogs, Dolby was founding director of the Computer and Information Science (CIS) Program on campus. In 1969, prior to the CIS's formation, Dolby began teaching a course called "Documentation and Information Retrieval" for the Department of Librarianship.

Given his reputation in the field, Dolby was chagrined by ALA's criticisms of the department's information science coursework, which in 1975 was part of the CIS Program. Declaring that he was "insulted" by ALA's decision not to reaccredit the library science program, Dolby wrote:

> I must admit that I am completely puzzled by the line of reasoning taken by the COA team in its response—pages 35-37—to the question of curriculum development and the role of the CIS Program in that development, particularly with regard to the teaching of information science. I remind you that I am a member of the American Library Association and the American Society for Information Science, that I have co-authored two well-regarded books on the use of computers in libraries and been principal investigator for three substantial studies for the U.S. Office of Education and two for the Library of Congress involving, again, the use of computers in libraries. And although I am quite happy in the math department at SJSU, I believe I could occupy a chair in most Schools of Librarianship and have turned down two such offers in the last several years. . . . I cannot for the life of me understand how our efforts could be dismissed so lightly. (Dolby to West, 20 March 1976, SLIS Archives)

Dolby had sent the above protest to Martha West, a library systems specialist who joined San José State's library science faculty in 1969. West had worked as a consultant for various Silicon Valley firms and played a pivotal role in developing the library systems coursework within the CIS Program. A consultant on numerous technology grant projects, West found ways to involve students in her work. For example, she was a member of Stanford's BALLOTS project, one of the earliest cooperative online cataloging efforts. Her students were given the opportunity to participate in this pioneering venture.[21]

---

[21] BALLOTS (Bibliographic Automation of Large Library Operations Through Time Sharing) was an early cooperative online cataloging project developed at Stanford in 1967.

West was also one of the earliest faculty members to consider how technology might be used to deliver instruction. One project she developed in 1972, called the "Micro-Readings Project," proposed putting class readings on microfiche. Students could check out fiche readers from the department office, she reasoned, and thus have "immediate around-the-clock access to course-related library materials" (Accreditation Review, 1978-1979, p. 252, SLIS Archives). At the time microform was the rising star of access systems, as West attested to in her grant proposal: "The Micro Book may in time become as important in academia as the paperback book; it is scarcely less revolutionary" (p. 252).[22]

After West left the department in 1978, her position was filled by Robert Dikeman, an online database expert with a PhD from Case Western Reserve. Dikeman's previous position was with Chemical Abstract Services, a pioneering database provider. In addition to teaching classes in online searching, Dikeman assisted other faculty in adding online components to their courses. Another new faculty hired to develop courses in online searching was Robert Wagers, who joined the department in 1976. With a BA in philosophy from San José State and both an MLS and a PhD in the history of science from the University of Oregon, Wagers was one of the earliest theoreticians on the faculty. He remained on the faculty for the next 30 years, providing key leadership for the department, most notably in its curriculum development. He served as interim department chair from 1983-1985.

Once the department had addressed its information science curriculum, it turned its attention to locating faculty to expand and enhance other professional specializations. Among the most important of these new hires was Clifford Johnson, who taught for SJSU from 1978 to 1989. Johnson had a long academic research library career, working as a reference librarian at the Claremont Colleges and the City University of New York, as well as serving as the librarian at the Ford Foundation. Terence Crowley also joined the faculty in 1978; his areas of expertise were reference and information and referral services. With an MLIS and PhD from Rutgers University, Crowley was highly regarded for his pioneering research in evaluating reference services. Indeed, Crowley was the first to report that reference librarians provided

[22] It is unknown whether this grant proposal was funded.

patrons with correct information 55% of the time, a landmark finding which influenced professional research for the next two decades. Crowley was also an award-winning teacher[23] notable for his reference courses, which taught generations of students how to critically use and evaluate reference sources. One assignment, popularly known as the "Word Project," became quite legendary, allowing students, as Crowley reflected, the "opportunity to show off their humor, originality, and artistry" (Crowley, 1998, p. 204).

Due to faculty resignations, retirements, and deaths, there was almost a complete turnover in library science faculty in the early 1980s. Elizabeth McClure Rosen was hired to handle the school library media program, Linda Main brought an expertise in information systems, Judith Tessier specialized in information organization and transfer, while Bill Fisher and Karen Ceppos had experience with academic and special libraries. These individuals would play a vital role in the program's development in coming decades.

The department also continued the tradition of including the current university librarian among its faculty, and between 1970 and 1988, three different library directors taught classes for the program. Stuart Baillie replaced Joyce Backus as library director in 1965 and began teaching courses in academic libraries and library management in 1969. He played an important role in San José State's bid for accreditation, supporting the department's efforts to expand the library's LIS collection to meet ALA standards. When Baillie stepped down as library director in 1977 to teach for the department full time, he was replaced by Harold Olsen. Formerly the director for planning and development at Oberlin College's library, Olsen was an expert in the economics of information. SJSU students also benefitted from the instruction of Maureen Pastine, who served as library director between 1980 and 1985, before accepting library director positions at Washington State, Southern Methodist, and Temple. Involved in the development of feminist studies during her tenure at SJSU, Pastine taught a course on Research Methods in Women's Studies.

SJSU also continued to hire promising young faculty who would make a professional name for themselves elsewhere. Two

[23] Crowley won the Association for Library and Information Science Education Award for Teaching Excellence in 1993.

of the more noteworthy of these sojourners were Robert Brundin and Suzanne Hildenbrand, both of whom became eminent LIS educators—Brundin at the University of Alberta's School of Library and Information Studies and Hildenbrand at the School of Library and Information Studies at the State University of New York, Buffalo. Jovanna Brown and Stephen Karetsky also taught temporarily for the department in the 1970s before embarking on academic library careers. Brown moved on to manage the library at Evergreen State College (Washington), becoming quite well known for her work with Native Americans and tribal libraries. Karetsky became the library director at Felician College (New Jersey) and has published extensively on such diverse topics as intellectual freedom, literacy, and automated library systems.

Finally, the department was geographically blessed by the rich professional community in the Silicon Valley and Bay Area, and the department's pool of part-time instructors significantly enhanced its course offerings. Of particular importance were instructors drawn from the local computer industry who played an invaluable role in developing SJSU's information science and library systems coursework. These included Dr. Neal Kaske, of UC Berkeley's Library Systems Office; Brian Aveny, Product Manager, Information Design Inc. of Menlo Park; Mark Baer, Hewlett-Packard Corporation Library Manager; and Karen Tackle-Quinn, Senior Librarian and Information Specialist at IBM. Other local librarians who most notably taught for the department for many years include Warren Hicks (library director at Chabot College), Edwin Tyson (reference librarian at San José City College), and Janice Lieberman (cataloger at Stanford Art Museum).

Perhaps the most distinguished of these part-time faculty was Bela H. Banathy, who taught classes at San José State from 1968-1971. A Hungarian immigrant who spent World War II in an Austrian refugee camp, Banathy was an expert in systems design. Before coming to San José State, he served as the Director of the Foreign Language Division of the U.S. Army Defense Language Institute in Monterey. While teaching for San José State, he was also employed as research director at the Far West Laboratory in San Francisco, where he did systems modeling for educational, social, and public service programs. Also an ordained minister, Banathy was working on the Agora Project at the time of his death in 2003, a worldwide effort to develop and use open-source software to stimulate political dialog among the general public (Muhlberger, 2005).

Between 1968 and 1988, the San José State library science faculty underwent a remarkable transformation. Until the late 1960s, almost all instructors specialized in school librarianship and curriculum materials, reflecting California's statewide mandate to prepare teacher-librarians. After 1968 the faculty became increasingly diverse to cover a range of library specializations and emerging information technologies. Moreover, new full-time faculty now had PhDs, signifying another major shift from previous decades. Situated in the heart of the Silicon Valley, the department—soon to become the Division of Library and Information Science—benefitted from an abundance of expertise in computing and information systems. These pioneering full- and part-time faculty members would modernize the department's curriculum and position it for the innovative work to come.

Students

As San José State's library science program diversified, student numbers increased substantially. By the mid-1970s, there were well over 200 students in the program, peaking at 288 students in the fall of 1976. However, this profusion of students proved short-lived. Although the department's accreditation problems affected admissions somewhat,[24] the real blow came from passage of California Proposition 13, a state initiative limiting property tax increases to 2% a year. Passed in June 1978, Prop 13 severely curtailed public, school, and academic library funding, thereby causing library jobs to plummet. According to Cindy Mediavilla (2008), California libraries lost over $35 million in funding, necessitating a 21% reduction in library staff (p. 19). Given this discouraging employment scenario, library science applications declined in 1979 by 44%. As the department's annual report explained:

---

[24] During this time, the department sent each applicant a letter concerning its accreditation status and the progress of its appeal.

> The uncertainty of the Division's accredited status and the unfavorable employment situation in the state prompted many persons, who would have applied for a Library Science degree objective, to select some other professional area of study, or choose to delay entry into the program until after the problem of accreditation was solved and the job situation stabilized. (Accreditation Review, 1978-1979, p. 85, SLIS Archives)

Although this was among the most challenging periods for SLIS faculty and students, it also produced some of the school's most notable alumni. The 1976-1978 cohort included Ann Caputo (1976), long-time executive with the Dialog and Dow Jones corporations and 2009 president of the Special Library Association; George Plosker (1977), another prominent figure in the Silicon Valley's database industry; Bonnie Buckley (1977), who established the Center for the Book as part of her work for the Nevada State Library; William Post (1977), an academic librarian who became Vice Provost and Chief Information Officer at California State University, Chico; Sarah Buchanan (1978), who went on to earn a doctorate and teach at the University of Pittsburgh School of Information Science; and Steve Fjeldsted (1978), a poet and author who became director of the South Pasadena Public Library (40 for 40 Alumni Celebration, 2007, SLIS Archives).

The department rebounded in the 1980s with student numbers rising every year. In the fall of 1985, more than 160 students were now in the program. By 1989 that figure had more than doubled, with enrollments reaching an impressive 345 students.

Before 1970, San José State's Department of Librarianship records did not pay much attention to the composition of this student body, probably because the students remained pretty much the same. As the department's 1974 annual report noted, "Prior to accreditation in 1969, the student body was a fairly homogeneous group composed primarily of women in their thirties, many of whom had prior teaching experience" (Self-Study Report, 1974, p. 162, SLIS Archives). Responding to the social movements of the 1970s, the department began aggressively recruiting a more diverse group of students, attending job fairs, speaking to ethnic studies classes, and participating in on-campus recruiting events. As a result of these efforts, the program's diversity improved somewhat. Data collected in the fall of 1979 showed that 71% of entering students were white; 10% were Latino; 10% were Asian American; 6% were African American; and 3% were Native American (Annual Report, 1979-1980, p. 70, SLIS Archives). Unfortunately for statistical purposes, in the 1980s, SJSU removed questions regarding race and ethnicity from its application form to comply with state affirmative action laws, so progress in this area is nearly impossible to track.

In most other areas, SJSU's library science students remained much the same. The gender ratio was consistently 85% female and 15% male, which was typical of the profession at that time. The majority of library science students continued to take courses part-time; in fact this characteristic of the program became even more pronounced during this period. In 1971, 55% of the students were part time; by 1985, 70% were part time. SJSU embraced these part-time students, making their educational needs central to the department's mission and goals. As the school explained to the ALA in 1985:

> The Division has always had students who fulfill the degree requirements on a part-time basis because of employment commitments or family responsibilities. To accommodate these individuals nearly half of the classes have always been scheduled in late afternoon or evening hours. In addition, the summer school schedule is designed to enable a student to complete most of the degree requirements by attending Summer Sessions only. Schedule flexibility has been considered one of the great strengths of the Division; it appeals to mature adults changing careers and to those seeking continuing education. (Self-Study Report, 1985, p. 143)

Despite the high number of part-time students, student life was spirited, though very different from the Bibliophiles of previous decades. The late 1960s and early 1970s was a turbulent era at San José State, a time in which the campus routine was disrupted with large, sometimes violent marches and sit-ins. The social activism began in

1968 with faculty-student protests against the pervasive discrimination against African American students, but then expanded to encompass other racial groups and the antiwar movement. The student uprising culminated in May 1970 with a campus-wide strike denouncing the US invasion of Cambodia. On May 18, the Faculty Senate lent its support to the movement, voting to cease teaching classes for the remainder of the academic year (Walsh, 2003, p. 37).

Library science students were very much a part of this campus turmoil, and the prevailing ideas and ethos shaped their departmental concerns and involvement. In 1970, students in the department formed "Concerned Library Students" (CLS) and demanded a wider role in departmental governance (Self-Study Report, 1974, p. 165, SLIS Archives). The CLS described themselves as "a group of library science students concerned about social, school, and community problems, and who meet together to see what, if anything, can be accomplished through group action" (*Student Guide*, n.d., p.1).

The CLS gave students an independent voice in departmental affairs. The CLS officers sat on departmental committees and attended faculty meetings. They had the right to write up formal statements regarding instructors which were added to faculty personnel files. CLS could also place discussion topics on faculty meeting agendas. During the Cambodian Crisis and general strike, CLS representatives met with library science faculty to determine whether to participate in the general campus shut down. Instead of cancelling classes, they decided to sponsor a series of lectures and films to shed light on the situation and explore ways in which libraries might become involved in the antiwar movement (Accreditation Review, 1969-1970, SLIS Archives).

The CLS was socially as well as politically active and sponsored various outreach programs for students to become more involved in the community. "Operation Elmwood," for example, was a CLS project to collect books for prisoners, while "Operation Read" involved students in a literacy program sponsored by the Santa Clara County Library System. Other socially conscious CLS activities included a tutoring service for foreign students and creating a special collection on minorities for the university library. In the spring of 1971, the CLS joined ALA's Social Responsibilities Round Table.

Though student activism waned by the mid-1970s, the CLS continued to function as the department's official student organization, sponsoring various on-campus activities and events. They issued a *Student Guide*, which gave new students pointers on what services were available and on how best to navigate the program. For example, in regards to parking, they advised:

> Parking is a problem especially at the beginning of the semester. There is a 25¢ a day parking lot directly opposite the Library on 4th Street. Arrive early. Prepare for a five to fifteen minute wait in line for a space.

As for typewriters, required technology since the 1930s, students could rent them in the library. "These machines are usually unsatisfactory," the CLS warned, "but may be suitable for last-minute chores. If you rent a typewriter from a local store, be sure to ask for the student discount" (*Student Guide*, n.d., pp. 3-4).

The CLS also worked to develop a sense of community by furnishing a student lounge, hosting a speaker's series, coordinating a textbook exchange and ride-share program, and publishing an occasional newsletter, called *Headnotes* in the early1970s and *The Water Mark* after 1978. In 1971, the CLS also helped create a San José State chapter of Beta Phi Mu, an international honor society for library science graduates.

Through these efforts the CLS sought to "give library students a chance to get to know each other and to be kept up to date on the happenings in the library science department." The CLS recognized the transitory nature of a part-time student body and sought to make a difference. "Many of us rarely see each other," observed *The Water Mark*'s editor in April 1978. "Night students seldom have a chance to feel like a part of the department. We hope our newsletter will help solve some of these problems" (p.1).

Concerned Library Students disappeared in the 1980s, but the organization helped the department weather the turbulent 1970s. It served as a mouthpiece for students whose careers were threatened by the accreditation crisis. It also developed a sense of community and school pride as San José State's library science program recouped in the

1980s. The CLS recognized the essential character of San José State's library science students and strove to find ways for them to connect with one another and with the community around them.

Summer Workshops and the Extension Program

During the early-1970s, San José State's continuing education efforts dealt primarily with programming for school librarians and media specialists. Organized and administered by faculty member Irene Norell, these programs reflected Norell's particular interest in library services for underrepresented populations. Norell's first institute was in the summer of 1969. Funded by Title II B of the Higher Education Act, the program was titled "Using Oral Communication to Expand Library Services for Children and Young People in Culturally Different Areas." Later that summer, Norell organized another grant-funded workshop titled "The Elementary School Library as Media Center." Despite its traditional sounding name, the program was taught in North Fork, California, and focused on developing school library media programs for Indian children living in the district. Over the next decade Norell and other faculty members hosted other socially conscious workshops and institutes, such as Recruitment and Training of the Disadvantaged as Library Personnel; Unions in Libraries: Collective Bargaining; and Library Outreach to the Unserved.

In the late 1970s and throughout the 1980s, the department played an important role in developing continuing education programs to introduce the profession to new library technologies. In 1980, for example, the department sponsored different extension courses in Dialog Systems, BRS Basic, ORBIT IV, and Micrographics in the Library (Annual Report, 1979-1980, pp. 19-20). The department also established an off-site program at Stanford Research Institute in Palo Alto. Here, faculty taught courses in computers and technology as well as classes in science and technology reference.

The success of these off-site programs clearly demonstrated that the local library community was counting on San José State to provide leadership in both the training and retooling of information professionals. The department already had experience teaching school library media courses off-site in the 1950s and 1960s. In the 1970s, a broader range of library science classes were taught off-site in such far-flung locations as Millbrae, Fresno, Monterey, and Bakersfield. As the 1980s came to an end, extension classes were becoming central to SJSU's education program and key to its self-identity. This commitment to delivering professional education beyond the university's boundaries would shape the program's destiny in the decades to follow.

Conclusion

When the Department of Librarianship was accredited by the ALA in 1969, it was a comprehensive library science program in name only. Despite accreditation and economic woes, the department spent the next two decades expanding its faculty and modernizing its curriculum to keep pace with social and technological changes. In the process, the program forged strong alliances with the professional community in the region and experimented with new modes of course delivery. The department was committed to offering professional education to any qualified student, regardless of personal circumstances. This democratic ideal provided the foundation of the program's continued expansion in the 1990s and beyond.

Chapter 6

Conveniently Located Everywhere: Educating Information Professionals throughout California and Beyond, 1989-2009

> But perhaps the most interesting lesson is that new growth, as in nature, emerges from the old. The distance education programs are a new growth, offering new educational opportunities in our field as we lose programs with long and honored traditions. . . . And as we move to renew and recreate, we make our education more responsive to human need. There is no more honorable objective.

—James Healey
SLIS Director
1991[25]

This final chapter of SLIS's history chronicles the program's transformation in the 1990s and early 2000s. SJSU's success during this period is quite remarkable given the obstacles it overcame and the failures of library science programs elsewhere. Yet when one reflects on SLIS's enduring features—its entrepreneurial character, respect for student needs in program planning, and ability to exploit new

[25] Healey, J. S. (1991). Distance library education. *Library Trends, 39* (4), 439-440.

technology for curriculum ends—SJSU's achievements are not so surprising after all.

As the 1990s opened, information professionals confronted complex challenges to the traditional workplace. The electronic library envisioned by SLIS professor Ken Dowlin in 1984 had come of age, requiring an entirely new set of professional theories and skills. Some believed that libraries were outmoded and librarianship a dying profession. As a 1995 article in the *Los Angeles Times* declared, computers were supplanting librarians' "beloved card catalogs" and "soon may replace libraries as we know them." The *Times* reporter predicted that "despite the thrill of physically browsing through books, ultimately we'll forget about the traditional library. . . . Instead, we'll simply message a librarian to send the book over the Internet" (Gest, 1995, pp. 26-27).

Adding credibility to the media's grim prognosis was that many library science programs downsized in the 1980s and early 1990s. In fact, between 1978 and 1995 no fewer than 18 LIS schools closed, accounting for more than 25% of the library science programs in the country. Library science programs in California had started disappearing even earlier. The library school at Immaculate Heart College closed in 1972; California State University, Fullerton's (CSUF) program ended in 1978; and the University of Southern California (USC) lost its school in 1986.[26] In the early 1990s, the library and information science programs at UCLA and UC Berkeley were under siege as well. UCLA's MLIS program survived by merging with the School of Education in 1994. That same year UC Berkeley dropped its MLIS program, becoming the School of Information Management and Systems, now known as the iSchool.

Happily, libraries did not succumb at this time, but instead rebounded in dramatic fashion. As they did, the popular media completely reversed itself and began touting librarianship as a thriving field. "Demand for Librarians Hits an All-Time High," proclaimed a 1999 article in the *National Business Employment Weekly* (Francois, 1999), while a 2000 issue of the *Occupational Outlook Quarterly* promoted librarians as "information experts in the information age" (Crosby, 2000, p. 3).

[26] The programs at Immaculate Heart and CSUF were unaccredited, while USC was accredited.

San José State's library and information science program, which had survived the pessimistic 1980s, now capitalized upon the profession's newfound energy. With its openness to flexible scheduling and its tradition of using the latest technologies to enhance and distribute course content, SLIS was ready to pioneer an entirely new mode of professional education.

Distance Education

From its earliest days, SLIS experimented with extended education as a way to provide professional training to employed teachers and library paraprofessionals. Beginning with summer school courses in the 1930s and 1940s, and branching out to different locations in the 1950s and 1960s, by the 1970s, San José State was graduating the majority of California's school librarians as well as a considerable number of librarians in other specializations. During the 1980s, SLIS went further afield by offering courses as far away as Fresno, Sacramento, and Bakersfield. For the most part, these off-site programs were ad hoc and opportunistic, depending on the availability of a supportive library host, qualified faculty, and enough students to make it cost effective. Ever mindful of potential accreditation problems, SLIS never allowed students to take more than seven off-site courses. To accommodate these commuting students, SLIS developed a "week-end university" and offered popular courses on Friday nights and Saturdays.

When the University of Southern California closed its library and information science program in 1986, suddenly the Los Angeles basin faced a severe shortage of degreed librarians. UCLA sponsored the region's one remaining professional program, but limited its admissions to full-time students only. Not only was there an insufficient local pool to fill current needs, it was too costly for libraries to pay for out-of-state job applicants to travel to California for interviews. Therefore, many Southern California libraries were forced to hire individuals without the MLIS degree. Even if these new library employees desired to pursue a professional degree, few educational options were available.

It was at this point that SLIS began planning a more ambitious off-campus program to meet the state's growing need for degreed librarians.

The goal was to create a statewide library and information science program, starting with courses in Fresno and Sacramento in the spring of 1988, then expanding to Sonoma in the fall of 1988, Los Angeles in the spring of 1989, and finally San Diego in the spring of 1990. Instructors would be drawn from the local professional community, while SLIS's regular faculty were expected to teach one course at a distant site every two years. There would be a three-year guarantee of operation at each site, unless the program suffered severe financial hardship. In this plan outlined in SLIS's 1987-1988 report to the ALA, students could still only take seven classes off-site. This limitation was written into ALA's accreditation guidelines, a point the ALA reiterated in its 1988 SLIS accreditation review (Annual Accreditation Report, 1987-1988, p. 2, SLIS Archives).

When SLIS announced its expansion plans, librarians in Southern California began lobbying for a more ambitious program to meet their meets. In November 1987, Serena Stanford, SJSU's Associate Vice President for Graduate Studies and Research, met with library directors at the California Library Association conference and learned firsthand about their difficulty recruiting suitable employees. Pat Bril, associate librarian at CSUF, was at this meeting and suggested to Dean Stanford that CSUF be considered as the Southern California "hub." Upon her return to Fullerton, Bril put Stanford in contact with CSUF's Associate Vice President of Academic Affairs, Dennis Berg, and the two campuses began to seriously consider establishing a SLIS branch at Fullerton (Stanford to Berg, 4 August 1988, SLIS Archives). CSUF was willing to gamble on SJSU's statewide plan, and the Southern California program opened in the fall semester of 1989 (Klassen to [CSUF] Long Range Planning and Priorities Committee, 30 March 1989, CSUF Archives).

Initially, SLIS committed only two years to the CSUF campus. It was self-supporting, so that student fees paid for all operating costs. After two years, SLIS faculty hoped that the library school could be transferred to CSUF to become an official academic unit on that campus. If not, then the Fullerton program would be "enfolded" into SJSU and become a state-funded operation. If neither of these scenarios occurred, SLIS's Fullerton program would be eliminated (Annual Accreditation Report, 1990-1991, p. 8).

From the outset SLIS's off-site program faced serious challenges. First, there was the expense, and the fact that Southern California students were paying so much more for the same education students received in San José. In addition, SLIS had no official status on the CSUF campus so that students and faculty had to negotiate SJSU's bureaucracy from afar. At Fullerton, SLIS required offices, classrooms, clerical support, and access to library resources and technology, all of which took time and money to get in place. Particularly worrisome, SLIS was scheduled for its ALA accreditation review in 1992, and there were concerns that the Fullerton program could hurt SLIS's reaccreditation bid. Then there was suspicion among some in the library community that quality professional education could not be conducted at a distance.

SLIS Director Healey aggressively confronted these issues as his ambitious distance education plan progressed. He kept the ALA apprised of the CSUF developments and raised the possibility with ALA officials that accreditation might be transferred from one university to another. He met early on with the library directors of the California State University System to solicit their support, and published an "Open Letter to the California Library Community" in the October 1988 *CLA Newsletter*. Hoping to preempt anticipated criticism, Healey's letter argued that "while some more traditional library school faculty cling to the idea that off campus education is, per se, academically suspect, the reality in the field apparently favors the development of off-campus programs throughout the nation." Healey pointed out that the schools of library and information science in Texas and Indiana already operated successful distance education programs without "diminishing" their reputations. "And with the University of Illinois seeking to establish a program in Chicago," Healey concluded, "one would have to believe that off campus education may be the wave of the future, and wonder why more schools do not engage in this important activity" (Healey, 1988, p. 9).

In contrast to the structural obstacles it faced, SLIS's Fullerton program enjoyed enthusiastic support from librarians throughout Southern California. CSUF proved to be an ideal institutional base, for not only was it a sister CSU campus with compatible administrative structures, its library had built a suitable library and information science collection when its own degree program was in operation.

CSUF allowed SLIS the use of its classrooms and office space, sold library science textbooks in its bookstore, and gave SJSU students and faculty library privileges. CSUF Librarian Richard Pollard and Associate Librarian Pat Bril faithfully represented SLIS interests on campus and forcefully argued for the importance and value of this new venture. Initially CSUF administrators expressed some reluctance to sponsor a degree controlled by another university. In a 1989 memorandum, Vuryl Klassen, chair of CSUF's Graduate Education Committee, asked CSUF's Long Range Planning and Priorities Committee if it was wise to allow "a student to graduate from San José State University while never attending one class on their campus" (30 March 1989, CSUF Archives). Pollard, who had been copied on the memorandum, responded in the affirmative. While acknowledging that residency was a troubling issue, Pollard argued that "in an era of tightening educational budgets, however, I believe that this innovative approach to meeting educational demand is worth a two-year experiment" (Pollard to John Olmstead, 4 April 1989, CSUF Archives).

Other Southern California libraries provided essential support to SLIS's Southern California program as well. Some libraries gave employees time off to attend classes, their staff spoke at SLIS-CSUF classes and events and supervised interns, while several institutions developed special scholarships to support graduate study. Pasadena Public Library's contribution was particularly noteworthy. In addition to Library Director Edward Szynaka vigorously promoting SJSU's early organizing and offering the free use of his library's classroom space, in 1989 the Pasadena Public Library Foundation awarded SLIS a $21,000 grant to get the CSUF program started. "We are very concerned about the lack of opportunities for working librarians who want to attend library school," the Foundation explained. "Since San Jose is prepared to take a leadership role by making more opportunities available, the Pasadena Public Library Foundation is prepared to support your efforts" (DLIS Bulletin, 1991-1992, p. 6). The Pasadena Public Library offered additional monetary support in subsequent years, including a $5,000 grant in 1991 and a $45,000 grant in 1993.

Another important source of on-going support was the Office of Library Affairs at the California State University Chancellor's Office. Director Tom Harris and Associate Director Gordon Smith both championed SLIS's Southern California efforts, even making available their own computing lab for SLIS courses. In a 1991 report to the Council of Library Directors of the California State University System, Associate Director Smith advocated for SJSU's library science expansion. "The quality of library services in California is threatened by a serious shortage of opportunities in professional library education," Smith warned, and "the three existing programs offering the Master of Library Science Degree cannot meet present and expected demand." Noting that "San José State's Fullerton MLS program has exceeded all expectations in its ability to attract students," Smith urged CSU library directors to support SJSU's plan to become a statewide library science program (pp. ii, 12).

Because of this strong local interest and support, SLIS's Fullerton program was an instant success. Four courses were offered in the fall of 1989, all filled to capacity. In fact, there were 171 enrollments that first semester, double the number expected.[27] In the following semester, there were 201 enrollments, and a year later this figure had risen to 377. The number of class offerings increased correspondingly, so that by the fall of 1992, 22 SJSU library science courses were being taught at CSUF.

Notwithstanding SLIS's success, California was hit hard with another economic downturn in the early 1990s, which thwarted the original plan to regularize the Southern California program. Over the next two years the California State University System's budget was reduced by more than 20%, causing individual campuses to be leery of developing new programs. Thus when SJSU's Graduate Dean Serena Stanford asked CSUF administrators in the spring of 1990 to take over the library school, they were reluctant to do so given the associated costs. While the university did philosophically agree that another library science program was needed in Southern California, no specific individual or department stepped forward to sponsor it at CSUF. Explained CSUF's Vice President for Academic Affairs Michael Clapp to Dean Stanford, "The combination of the State's uncertain budgetary future (both 1990-91 and beyond) and the apparent lack of strong faculty interest here make Fullerton's long-term involvement in

[27] Enrollments refer to the total number of students in all classes. A student taking two classes counts as two enrollments.

this endeavor ambiguous at best" (Clapp to Stanford, 27 June 1990, SLIS Archives).

The CSUF program suffered a second blow when the CSU Chancellor's Office determined that it had no money to fund the Fullerton program and would not consider SLIS's proposal for another three to five years (Annual Accreditation Report, 1990-1991, p.8, SLIS Archives). Faced with closing its Fullerton campus, where enrollments now exceeded 700, SLIS faculty voted to extend it as a self-funded program for two more years. As Director Healey explained to the ALA in SLIS's 1992 accreditation report:

> We recognize that the situation in which we, the Division and the University, find ourselves is indeed a sticky one. We had originally intended to operate the program for two years in a self-support system, after which we expected the California State University System to assume the costs. But in that second year the state's budget situation worsened, and has continued downward since . . . . We were obviously meeting needs, and decided we could not in good conscience walk away from our [Fullerton] program. (Self- Study Report, 1992, p.4-5, SLIS Archives)

The next two years were transformative in the history of SLIS's distance education. While the ALA did reaccredit SJSU's library science program in 1992, it expressed concerns about conditions at CSUF that had to be addressed. The ALA also indicated that it could not guarantee the automatic transfer of accreditation from one university to another, should CSUF or some other state university campus be willing to adopt the Southern California program. At the same time, the CSUF program, because it was not dependant on state funds, continued to grow and prosper. Student fees not only allowed SLIS to hire a full-time associate director and three full-time faculty members for the CSUF campus, but also paid for a fully outfitted computer lab and student lounge, as stipulated by the ALA in its 1992 review. Indeed, SLIS's Southern California operation was so successful that

SLIS began teaching classes in other Southern California locations, such as Pasadena, San Diego, and Palm Springs.

Having demonstrated its value and viability, the CSUF program, by 1992, was attracting the interest of several nearby state universities, including Cal Poly Pomona and Cal State San Bernardino. At CSUF, San José's program had forged a strong alliance with the Computer Science Department. Its chair, David Falconer, envisioned incorporating library science into the Computer Science Department to create a new and innovative "information/media degree"(The Fullerton Program: A Five Year Plan, [27 May 1992], p. 1, SLIS Archives). Indeed, the success at CSUF prompted librarians at UC Riverside to submit to the University of California a proposal to open a library science program there (Proposal for a Graduate School , 1991, SLIS Archives).

But the mood on SJSU's campus had changed. SLIS Director Healey now fought the plan to turn over the CSUF program to some other institution. Claiming that distance education was "easily operated" out of SJSU,[28] Healey argued that SLIS should resuscitate its original plan to create a statewide library science program (Healey to Stanford, 2 July 1992, p. 2, SLIS Archives). In a memorandum submitted to Dean Stanford in May 1993, Healey proposed that SLIS retain its Southern California "anchor" at CSUF and then set up additional "hubs" at other state universities. At the same time he reflected on what SLIS had accomplished:

> The creation of the Southern California program, which I hope will serve as the prototype of the statewide effort, has been an arduous, and at times, a terribly frustrating experience. Yet because we persevered, we have seen the results of our efforts in the faces of those receiving degrees in their chosen profession. Those faces are strong testament to the worth of our work. (17 May 1993, SLIS Archives)

---

[28] Credit must be given to the administrative skills of SLIS associate directors Bill Fisher and Nancy Burns.

When Healey resigned as SLIS director in July 1993, the implementation of SLIS's statewide library school fell to his successor, Stuart Sutton. SLIS's new director refined and expanded Healey's original plan, adding a significant technological component to it. Sutton commended Healey for having "the guts" to respond to the "southern California library community's outcry for educational opportunities." He also agreed with his predecessor that "cloning" one program to start a new one was "no longer feasible." Not only were the costs and accreditation issues insurmountable, but equally important, a new educational paradigm had emerged where, to quote Sutton, "the boundaries of place and distance" were less important than "the demands of time and access" (Sutton to Robinson and Stanford, 3 September 1994, SLIS Archives; Sutton, 1993).

Sutton's first task was to develop "A Plan for Statewide Technology-Mediated Distance Education." After it was approved by SLIS faculty in August 1993, Sutton sought to use interactive video technology and the Internet to bring LIS classes to multiple sites. A brilliant spokesman for the educational possibilities of new communication technologies, Sutton secured several large grants that paid for videoconferencing facilities to be built at SJSU and CSUF. The most substantial was a $3 million grant awarded by PacBell in August 1994 to purchase and install high-end two-way interactive video equipment at SJSU, CSUF, and other participating state universities (Sutton, 1996, p. 823). Sutton also secured smaller grants to improve SLIS's classroom, offices, and lab space at CSUF.

The new broadcasting facilities were completed by late 1994 and the first three interactive video classes were taught between SJSU and CSUF in the spring of 1995. Thereafter, between five and ten video classes were scheduled each semester, first between Fullerton and San José; then as the retrofitting continued, hookups were made with Sonoma State, Sacramento State, San Francisco State, and Fresno State. Concurrently, SLIS faculty commuted to teach classes at Cal State San Marcos and Cal State Northridge. SLIS was truly becoming a statewide library science program.

SLIS's statewide video network was in full operation when Blanche Woolls assumed the school's directorship in 1997. A distinguished professor from the University of Pittsburgh, Woolls's reputation and expertise was in school libraries and children's literature, not emerging information technologies. Yet she understood the potential of SLIS's distance education program and envisioned it becoming entirely virtual in the very near future. At that time, the SLIS faculty was already experimenting with a different format to teach their distance classes. Called "hybrid" or "mixed mode" classes, these consisted of several in-person class meetings, with online instruction that took place in between. This mixed mode concept proved quite popular with students and faculty for it allowed them to retain the important interpersonal connections forged in face-to-face classes, yet took advantage of the convenience of asynchronous learning via the Web. As faculty gained confidence teaching in an online environment, they gradually reduced the number of on-site meetings for their hybrid classes from five to three to, in some cases, only one in-person session during the semester.

SLIS offered its first fully online courses in the spring of 2001: an online searching class (LIBR 240) taught by Nancy Burns and an advanced management course (LIBR 282) taught by Barbara Leonard. Burns and Leonard were former part-time faculty who had moved out of state, so the online courses were an appealing opportunity both for them and their students. The next fall several other faculty members put their courses on the Web: Adele Fasick, Resources for Children, 7-12; Taylor Willingham, Adult Literacy Services; and Janine Stanhope, Advanced Web Design. In the fall of 2005, the CSUF campus was teaching only three face-to-face classes, all of which were interactive video. In contrast, there were 26 online and 26 hybrid courses on CSUF's schedule. Interactive video classes were phased out by 2007. By that time 84% of what were now called "special session" courses were being taught completely online.

Students living near San José were similarly eager to take online and hybrid courses, even though they had the option of attending traditional classes on campus. In the fall of 2005, only 6 weekly classes were offered at SJSU; the remaining 46 were equally divided between online and hybrid. Two years later, only 2 weekly on-site courses were offered compared to 22 hybrid ones. The number of online courses had jumped to 71.

As Stuart Sutton had predicted in 1993, geography ceased to be a determining factor in LIS education as SLIS students increasingly opted for online classes. The online format erased tangible and intangible differences between SLIS's on-site and off-site courses. Faculty could teach their specialties to all students regardless of where they lived, and regular and special session students intermingled in courses on an equal basis. Online courses successfully blended the on-site and off-site programs, making it possible for SLIS to fulfill its vision of becoming "one team, one School." In March 2009, SLIS faculty decided to stop teaching in-person, on-site courses altogether. The school closed its Fullerton office—whose functionality had gradually disappeared—and publicly announced that in the fall of 2009, SLIS would become an entirely virtual MLIS program. Reflecting this new vision was a new motto; SLIS was now a "Global eCampus in Library and Information Science."

Curriculum

Faced with declining students and threatened closure, library schools struggled in the 1990s to reinvent themselves. Library and information science educators responded to the crisis by reasserting the profession's relevance in an information economy and identifying the new roles an information professional might play. In California, administrators of the state's three library and information science programs formed a "CLA Task Force on the Future of the Library Profession" to begin developing a new curricular focus. In a report submitted to the California Library Association in 1995, Stuart Sutton (SJSU), Nancy Van House (UC Berkeley), and Marcia Bates (UCLA) contended that librarianship was "in a period of rapid change" and competing "for its professional domain." To survive, they argued, schools of library and information science must identify their unique niche and revise their curriculum accordingly. In particular, LIS programs had to move beyond their traditional institutional focus (i.e., school libraries, public libraries, academic libraries, etc.) and develop a more theoretical curriculum built on specific values, tools, and areas of expertise (p.1).

Since the late 1980s, SLIS's curriculum had actually been moving in the opposite direction. During a series of meetings in 1986 and 1987, the faculty decided to emphasize the professional and technical components of library and information science education and make more room for hands-on learning through internships and projects. As Director Healey commented in a 1991 interview,

> When we rebuilt the program a few years ago we did some looking at that question and decided that our program was a professional one. We consider it our responsibility to educate people to practice the profession of librarianship, which we feel is a very honorable profession. We mix theory with practice. Unlike the other two schools in California, we are not a research institution, nor a research library school. We are a professional school. (p. 1)

As part of this curricular reconfiguration in the late 1980s, SLIS developed six different specializations reflective of employment opportunities in the state:

- Libraries and Information Organizations: Academic, Public, School, Special, Information Industry
- Services: Children's, Information Services
- Technology: Microcomputers, Automation, Online Services
- Database Development and Management
- Technical Services: Organization/Cataloging
- Management

Students were required to take five courses at the outset of their program: Information and Society, Reference and Information Services, Cataloging and Classification, Microcomputers in Libraries, and Management of Information Organizations. Thereafter, students were free to specialize in an area of their choice. At the end of their 42-unit program, students still had to pass a three-hour comprehensive exam.

Stuart Sutton brought a different curricular outlook when he replaced retiring James Healey as SLIS director in 1993. With expertise in intellectual property rights and the organization of information,[29]

[29] Sutton possesses a law degree as well as an MLIS and PhD.

Sutton proposed moving the curriculum back in a more theoretical direction and expanding its professional boundaries. He saw emerging interactive technologies as the key to pedagogical and curricular innovation, both of which marked his short career at SJSU (Sutton, 1996).

Sutton, thus, initiated another thoroughgoing curriculum review to ensure that the school's offerings were keeping pace with innovations in the information field. As a result of this review, classes in reference and cataloging were made elective rather than required, based on the argument that they represented professional specializations that not all librarians would pursue. LIBR 203, Microcomputers in Libraries, was dropped from the curriculum, since its content (how to use various software) was now common knowledge among the current generation of students. The new required core was reduced to three broad theoretical courses: Information and Society (LIBR 200), Organization of Information (LIBR 202), and Management of Information Organizations (LIBR 204). The goal of these courses was to "establish a predictable set of knowledge and skills upon which the advanced courses may build." They also covered professional/theoretical topics that faculty believed "all students should know regardless of their future job titles" (Program Presentation, 2000, p. 15). With fewer required courses, students were free to build greater expertise in their area of interest.

The faculty then tackled the program's exit requirement, the comprehensive exam. Traditionally, the exam was given on a Friday morning at the end of the semester. Taking place between 9 a.m. and 12 p.m., students were given a set of questions and asked to write spontaneously and at length on two of them. Essays were graded on a pass/fail basis. Typical of the comprehensive questions were this pair from the spring 1990 exam:

- How well are libraries doing in serving society's need to know and how must they change to respond to the demands of the next 20 years? And will they change?
- If a child, age 11, approached you at the children's desk (school or public library) and asked "Where are your books on Washington?" how would you help him?

Feeling that a one-time exam should not determine whether or not a student had rightfully earned an MLIS, the faculty instituted in its place the "Culminating Experience,"[30] or the CE as it was informally called. The CE was a full semester's course during which students wrote two 20-page research papers on topics submitted by the faculty. These topics ran the gamut of professional expertise covered within the SLIS curriculum. They were also, as the following examples show, an index to pressing professional issues of the day:

- A number of studies show that people's reading behavior is experiencing significant changes. It was argued that "current work in digital library design and development is participating in a general societal trend toward shallower, more fragmented, and less concentrated reading" (Levy, 1997). Discuss the following issues: (1) Factors contributing to the changes in reading behavior; (2) Impacts of digital media on people's reading behavior. (Spring 2003)

- In April 2003, we watched the looting and burning of Iraq's National Library and Archives, National Museum, and other cultural heritage sites in the wake of the US occupation of Baghdad. What was the archival community's response to the destruction of Iraq's historical and archival collections and what actions did it take? Are there other examples in modern history (since 1900) of historical records being consciously destroyed? What do these incidents (including the most recent in Iraq) reveal about the role and significance of archives in society, culture, and politics? (Spring 2004)

- California school libraries are said to be some of the worst in the nation. Is this really true? First, using federal and state statistics, document this fact. Second, trace efforts made by CSLA, and other groups and individuals to turn this around in the last ten years. Finally propose a plan that individuals, groups,

[30] The name derived from the California State University's requirement that all master's degree students complete a culminating experience prior to graduation.

and organizations can implement to bring solid funding and support for school libraries in this state. (Fall 2004)

- According to a *Washington Times* article published on September 21, 2005, and written by Shaun Waterman, a data-mining intelligence team claims that they identified the 9/11 ringleaders as terrorists more than a year before the attacks. What is "data mining"? Trace the developmental history of data mining, and discuss its theoretical principle as well as technological elements. Explain how it's different from "text mining" and how it's related to the general field of information retrieval. (Spring 2006)

The CE, like all curricular requirements, reflected not only the current needs of the profession, but also the values and priorities of the school's current faculty and administration. Such was the case in 2005, when Ken Haycock succeeded the retiring Blanche Woolls as SLIS director. A prominent figure within the LIS community and an expert in program planning and assessment, Haycock encouraged SLIS faculty to articulate the school's overarching learning goals to better measure student learning. Under Haycock's guidance, SLIS faculty identified fourteen professional competencies that all SLIS students should possess when they graduate. Haycock then proposed that students create an electronic portfolio to showcase their expertise in these fourteen areas. Never fully satisfied with the previous CE process, the faculty quickly approved the e-Portfolio plan. It went into effect in the fall of 2006.

In lieu of the comprehensive exam, CE essays, or e-Portfolio, students always had the option of researching and writing an original master's thesis. Although a small minority of students choose the thesis option, their work represents the school's diverse student body and curriculum coverage. Indeed, thesis topics have ranged from the historical to the technological. Taken together they are interesting reflections of scholarly and professional issues and trends of their time:

- Barbara June Murray, "A Historical Look at the ALA Code of Ethics" (1990)

- Wynona Kimmel, "A Study to Identify Racial or Sexual Stereotypical Behavior in the Newbery Award Books " (1990)
- Roberta Corwin, "Gender Differences in the Library Computing Specialization" (1992)
- Richard Ward, "Copyright Law as Impacted by Changes in Computer Software Technologies" (1992)
- Elizabeth Rockefeller-MacArthur, "American Indian Library Services in Perspective: From Petroglyphs to Hypercard" (1993)
- Kenley Neufeld, "The Benefits of Electronic Communication among Library Professionals" (1994)
- Suellen Cox, "Student Use of CD-Rom Indexes at One Academic Library" (1994)
- Nensi Brailo, "Librocide: Destruction of Libraries in Croatia, 1991-1995" (1998)
- Joelle Mellon, "Most Glorious Mother: Images of the Virgin Mary in Women's Books of Hours" (1998)
- Cathy Lu, "Indochinese Students' Behavior in Using Academic Libraries: A Case Study" (2000)
- Debra Dvornik, "Digital Library Creators and Uses: Evaluating Intended Users versus Actual Users" (2004)
- T. Elizabeth Edwards, "Irreconcilable Allegiances: National Security Versus Intellectual Freedom" (2004)
- Rachel Wexelbaum, "The Use of Public Library Resources and Services during the 'Coming Out' Process" (2004)
- Daryl Fisher-Ogden, "The Library at Mission San Gabriel Arcangel" (2005)
- Jean Amaral, "The Impact of Televised Sports on Adult Nonfiction Sports Publishing" (2006)
- John Ridener, "From Polders to Postmodernism: An Intellectual History of Archival Theory" (2007)
- Nicole Hunter, "Documenting Variable Media Art: A Case Study" (2007)
- Trista Raezer, "Libraries in American German Prisoner of War Camps during World War II" (2008)
- David Gross, "Assessment of Information Literacy Instruction" (2009)

Indicative of the high-quality scholarship SLIS students have produced, two LIS theses were honored with the university's outstanding thesis award: Carol Moen Wing in 2002 for her study of Henry VIII's royal library, and April Gage in 2006 for her oral history of the Freedom to Read Foundation.

Since the late 1990s, SLIS's curriculum has remained stable, with curricular expansion focused on the development of new and/or updated professional specializations. In 1997, the school added an archival studies track. Since that time, specializations in the organization of information, reference services, information systems, and youth librarianship have been added or updated as well. Characteristic of Ken Haycock's innovative leadership, SLIS has become even more ambitious in its program development. In 2005, SLIS began an Executive MLIS program geared toward individuals already working in an information organization yet lacking the professional degree. More recently, SLIS inaugurated a new master's degree in Archives and Records Administration (MARA), the first of its kind in the nation. The school has also forged a unique partnership with Australia's Queensland University of Technology to offer a Gateway PhD program for American and Canadian students. The latter two programs accepted their first students in the fall of 2008. And despite the grim current economic climate, the future of both programs looks bright.

Faculty

This period of program growth and pedagogical experimentation shaped the composition and character of SLIS faculty in significant ways. Given its enviable location in the heart of the Silicon Valley, SLIS seized the opportunity to develop specializations relating to the telecommunications industry in the area and recruited faculty to forge those connections. Geoffrey Liu, for example, was hired by SLIS in 1995 to develop courses in programming and emerging information technologies. With a PhD in communications and information sciences from the University of Hawaii at Manoa, Liu worked with Linda Main to develop and maintain SLIS's information architecture specialization.

Ziming Liu was another new faculty hired partially for his connections with the information industry. Formerly a research scientist at Ricoh California Research Center, a digital imaging technology firm with headquarters in the Silicon Valley, he taught at the University of Washington before coming to San José State in 2000. Liu specializes in digital libraries and has published extensively on user behavior and reading in a paperless society.

Another important theme in SLIS's faculty development since 1989 was the need to create a distance faculty whose credentials and contributions to SLIS were commensurate with colleagues teaching at SJSU. To do otherwise would not only negatively impact the quality of the educational program at remote sites but jeopardize the reputation and accreditation status of the main campus program. SLIS Director Healey thus sought faculty for the CSUF campus possessing "credentials that made them eligible for faculty status in any library school in the United States" (Progress Report: The Southern California MLS Program, ca. 1990, SLIS Archives). Healey's original hires included William Aguilar (PhD, Illinois, 1983), who was University Library Director at CSU San Bernardino; Bonnie Rogers (PhD, Southern California, 1980), Dean of Learning Resources at Saddleback College; Debra Hansen (PhD, UC Irvine, 1988), who was history curator at the Anaheim Public Library; and Cecelia Wittman (PhD, University of Chicago, 1984), an information consultant and part-time instructor at UCLA. Aguilar and Rogers taught the Information and Society course (LIBR 200), Hansen covered Reference and Information Services (LIBR 201),Wittman handled Cataloging and Classification (LIBR 202), and Healey commuted to Fullerton to teach the required management course (LIBR 204). Healey and SLIS Associate Director Bill Fisher provided extensive advising and administrative direction in Southern California, as well.

Healey quickly determined that his teaching and administrative responsibilities were too demanding. Thus Gay Kinman was hired in the summer of 1990 to serve as the CSUF site's associate director. Kinman, who subsequently became a published novelist, was replaced by Nancy Burns (PhD, Southern California, 1986) the following year. Burns, who was working as an information broker and consultant in the Pasadena area, served as associate director until 1994, and her stable presence was an important ingredient in SLIS's successful distance education program at that time.[31]

A turning point in the history of SLIS's distance education program was the hiring of Judith Weedman and Debra Hansen, the first full-time tenure track faculty members assigned to teach at SLIS's Southern California campus. Having completed her PhD at the University of Michigan in 1989, Weedman taught at the University of California, Berkeley, and the University of Illinois prior to coming to SJSU. She brought with her an expertise in indexing and vocabulary design and has played a key role in the development of courses in these areas. At the same time, Hansen, who had been teaching for SLIS as a part-time faculty member since 1989, was hired as the second SLIS faculty sited at CSUF. With an MLIS from UCLA and a PhD in history from the University of California, Irvine, Hansen's assignment was to develop an archival studies track, which she did in 1996. Since then, several more faculty members have been hired by SLIS to teach from the Fullerton hub. These include Ken Dowlin (2000), an expert in public library administration; Dan Fuller (2002), who specializes in library automation and management; and Kristen Radsliff Clark (2007), whose area of concentration revolves around information literacies in children. As SLIS's distance education program evolved from on-site teaching at distant sites to teaching online courses, the pressure on SLIS to support a faculty contingent in Southern California subsided. Since the early 2000s, the program has been able to bring in faculty irrespective of where they plan to live or teach.

Another feature of SLIS's faculty development since 1990 has been the contributions made by former SJSU library directors. Both Ruth Hafter (SJSU Librarian, 1986-1992) and C. James Schmidt (SJSU Librarian, 1992-1999) joined the SLIS faculty upon leaving their administrative post in the library. Hafter had a long career as an academic librarian, serving as library director for Sonoma State University Library before coming to SJSU. Hafter contributed to the development of SLIS's management and academic libraries courses and was among the first faculty members to successfully teach courses via interactive video. Schmidt also brought an expertise in library

[31] Subsequent associate directors were Cindy Mediavilla (1994-1995), Debra Hansen (1995-2000), and Ken Dowlin (2000-2005).

administration to SLIS, but his major contribution has been in the area of intellectual freedom. Long a defender of freedom of information, Schmidt received numerous awards for his work, including the Robert B. Downs Intellectual Freedom Award from the University of Illinois (1991) and the Norwin S. Yoffie Career Achievement Award by the Northern California Chapter of the Society of Professional Journalists (2001). Upon his retirement in 2009, Schmidt was given the ALA Beta Phi Mu Award for his distinguished service to professional education.

Finally, among the most significant aspects of SLIS's faculty development in recent years has been the rejuvenation of the school libraries and youth services specializations. In the 1960s and 1970s, SLIS downplayed its past association with school libraries to build a curriculum in a broader range of fields. In the last decade, SLIS has reassumed its preeminence in this area through the hiring of a series of experts in school libraries and youth services. Most notable is David Loertscher, who joined SLIS's faculty in 1996. A prolific contributor to contemporary literature on school libraries, Loertscher revitalized SLIS's school library media credential program and achieved national recognition for his work. Indeed, in 2009, *US News and World Report* ranked SLIS's school library media program as fourth best in the country. Loertscher has not been alone in building this new youth-centered curriculum. Former SLIS director Blanche Woolls was well known in the school library field and gave strong support and credibility to SLIS's school library media program. Dan Fuller had also been a school librarian and consultant for Follett Educational Services prior to teaching for SLIS. Moreover, SLIS also expanded its expertise in youth services, hiring Anthony Bernier in 2005 and Joni Bodart the following year. With an MLIS from UC Berkeley and a PhD in history from UC Irvine, Bernier had attracted attention for his innovative work in young adult services, particularly in developing the acclaimed TeenS'cape Department at the Los Angeles Public Library. Since coming to SJSU Bernier has designed courses geared toward young adults as well as taught Information and Society and Research Methods offerings. Joni Bodart is an internationally recognized expert in booktalking, a technique to encourage children's recreational reading. Author of 20 books on booktalking and reader's advisory services more generally,

Bodart has restructured and expanded SLIS's Youth Librarianship specialization to better meet the current needs of that field.

During this period of unprecedented expansion, SLIS hired many part-time faculty to augment the teaching areas of its full-time faculty and meet the growing demand for classes. Initially, SLIS recruited prominent librarians living near San José or in the locations where off-site courses were taught. For example, SLIS classes in Sacramento were taught not only by regular faculty, but also by information professionals drawn from local public and school libraries, as well as the California State Library and California State Archives. San Diego-based courses drew faculty from the Fullerton hub as well as from academic, public, and special libraries in the vicinity.

As SLIS's online course offerings expanded, the school was able to hire faculty from a nationwide, indeed international pool. As SLIS noted in its 2007 accreditation report to the ALA, "While some local librarians with strong expertise in certain areas do teach for the School, most of our part-time faculty are drawn from a much wider environment, and bring national reputations to the School" (p.49). In fact, at that time, SLIS's part-time faculty boasted of five previous LIS deans and directors and 20 instructors teaching for other ALA-accredited library and information science programs.

Now that geography no longer limited SLIS's hiring, SLIS could hire faculty solely on the basis of their credentials. As a result, more and more part-time faculty had PhDs. In fact, currently, over 50% of SLIS's part-time faculty have doctorates in library and information science or in a discipline relevant to their teaching field. In addition to rising academic credentials, SLIS's part-time faculty is increasingly diverse, both in terms of ethnic and cultural background, and in professional and institutional affiliation. Faculty members reside throughout the United States, as well as in Canada, France, Ireland, and New Zealand. They work in a broad array of organizations ranging from prestigious universities like Yale and Stanford to Sun Microsystems and Boeing Aircraft Company. Part-time and full-time lecturers (most notably Debbie Faires, Lori Lindberg, Jeremy Kemp, and Lili Luo) have taken the lead in developing innovative coursework in emerging and immersive technologies. As a result of their path-breaking work, SLIS has been able to offer an array of courses covering topics such as

Web 2.0, Encoded Archival Description, Second Life and Immersive Worlds, even Gaming in Libraries.

The most influential faculty member recruited in recent years is Ken Haycock, who replaced the retiring director Blanche Woolls in 2005. A Canadian, Haycock earned a certificate in school librarianship from the University of Toronto (1971), an MLIS from the University of Michigan (1974), an EdD from Brigham Young University (1991), and an MBA from Royal Roads University (2004). During his distinguished career, Haycock has been employed in various academic and administrative positions and was director of the School of Library, Archival and Information Science, at the University of British Columbia from 1992 to 2002. He has played a prominent role in Canadian and American professional associations, serving as president for the Canadian Library Association (1977-1978), the American Association of School Librarians (1997-1998), and the Association for Library and Information Science Education (2005-2006). Publishing extensively on topics relating to library administration and school libraries, Haycock has also edited professional journals, such as *Teacher Librarian* and *Resource Links.* As noted earlier, at SJSU Haycock has spearheaded the creation of several groundbreaking new programs, most notably an Executive MLIS, a degree in archives and records administration (MARA), and a gateway PhD program through Australia's distinguished Queensland University of Technology. Under Haycock's leadership, SLIS was also granted a seven-year reaccreditation by the ALA in 2007.

Haycock's directorship, which built on the work of his predecessor, has brought the SLIS program full circle. Not only were Haycock and Woolls both former school library specialists, but each of their administrations was instrumental in the restoration of the school's prominence in school libraries and children's services. At the same time, SLIS continued to expand and diversify its curricular reach, inaugurating new specializations and degree programs in response to the exploding opportunities in the information professions. The numerical growth and financial success of SLIS has made it possible to hire a productive group of scholars to oversee the development of these new fields. Then, too, SLIS has been blessed with an incomparable pool of part-time faculty, who have added a level of curricular sophistication and breadth unimaginable when the school began 80 years ago.

Students

In 2008, the typical SLIS graduate was female (80%), white (67%), and a California resident (95%). Most likely taking classes part time, it took her three years to complete her degree and there was a 60% chance that she was working in a library during this time (Student Exit Survey, Fall 2008, SLIS Archives). According to this profile, the 2008 graduate did not look very different from SLIS students in the past, yet these statistics belie real changes, both subtle and dramatic, in the school's student body.

When SLIS opened its branch site in Fullerton in the fall of 1989, there were 290 students attending classes in San José. Then, as now, 80% of SLIS's students were female, attending classes part time. SLIS admissions stagnated in the early 1990s, the result of a poor state economy and the general concern over the future of librarianship as a profession. Yet, as the economy recovered, interest in librarianship sparked, and by 1999, SLIS's student body had nearly doubled. SLIS's development of hybrid and online classes made it possible for individuals in increasingly far-flung regions in California to take library science courses and, as a result, student admissions exploded. In fact, between fall 2001 and fall 2002, students enrolled in the program increased by 37% and by another 45% the following academic year. Student numbers have grown steadily since, and by the fall of 2008, nearly 2,800 were in the program, an increase of over 375%.

Beyond sheer numbers, online and hybrid courses encouraged more regional diversity among students. Whereas 98% of the students lived in California in 2000—equally divided between Northern California and Southern California—by 2008, 85% of SLIS students were California residents. Perhaps more telling is the geographical distribution of students living outside California. In 2000 only 2% of SLIS students came from out of state, and none were international. By contrast, the non-California students in 2008 hailed from 45 different states and 12 countries[32] (Biennial ALA Report, 2008, p. 9, SLIS Archives).

---

[32] The majority of international students were living in Canada. Others were from Denmark, Korea, China, Japan, the Philippines, South Africa, and the United Kingdom.

SLIS's student body is not only much larger and more geographically dispersed, it is also getting younger. In fall 1991, only 24% of the students were in their twenties, compared to 65% who were in their thirties and forties. By the fall of 2007, 65% of the students were now in their twenties and thirties. And while in 1991 31% of SLIS students were in their forties, in 2007, only 20% were in their forties. SLIS still had a respectable number of mature students. In fact, in 2007over 300 students were in their fifties and sixties.

Despite SLIS's unprecedented growth since 1989, much about the student body remains the same. As noted above, the vast majority are still Californians planning to work in the state's libraries and archives. The gender balance improved modestly, rising from a 84:16 female/male ratio in the 1980s to a 77:23 female ratio in 2007. Despite concerted effort by SLIS administrators to address the program's diversity, the ratio of ethnic to white students has declined. In a report submitted to the ALA in 1979, 71% of the students were listed as white. Twenty years later, in 1999, 79% of that year's graduates who listed their ethnicity were white. Among the 19% self-identifying themselves as an ethnic minority, Asian Pacific students constituted the largest ethnic group (10%), followed by Hispanics (5%), Native Americans (2%), and African Americans (2%). Another 2% were international students (ALISE Report, 1999, p. 6, SLIS Archives). This ethnic composition has remained about the same, despite the wider availability of the program through online courses. Although high compared to most LIS program, SLIS's 2007 report to the ALA indicated that still only 22% of its students identified themselves as minority (Program Presentation, 2007, p. 63).

SLIS's distributed student body has challenged traditional avenues of student action and culture. Yet student organizations have persisted—in some years even thrived—and through their extracurricular work they have sought to express student concerns and needs. After Concerned Library Students disappeared in the early 1980s, a new student group was formed in 1987/1988. Called L.I.S.S. (Library and Information Science Students), this organization had two stated goals: 1) "to be the 'official' forum and voice of the LIS student body that can formally (and informally) interface with the faculty and division chair;" and 2) "to be the forum for social events of/by/for the LIS student body"

(Guide for Incoming L.I.S.S. Officers, 1991, p. 1). During the 1990s, L.I.S.S. routinely sponsored a full range of on-campus events, including a new student orientation, the annual convocation, a lunch-time speaker's series, and receptions with representatives from professional associations. L.I.S.S. also organized tours of interesting libraries, both nearby (such as to NASA/Ames, Dialog, and Redwood Public Library [named Library of the Year in 1992]) and further afield (including the State Railroad Museum and the State Library in Sacramento). L.I.S.S. also provided a number of on-campus services, managing student lockers and mailboxes as well as a fully equipped student lounge.

L.I.S.S. started its newsletter in 1988. Initially called the *L.I.S.S. Newsletter*, it morphed into *UL: The Underground Librarian* by 1991. Despite its name, the *UL* covered the accustomed information about the organization's officers and events. It also contained miscellaneous news items, such as when lab fees were due ($25 per class in 1990), an editor's note, and library-related cartoons.

As SLIS ceased to be a traditional campus-based program in the late 1990s, L.I.S.S. fell on hard times. In fact, by 1995, faculty meeting minutes commented on increasing student apathy for L.I.S.S.'s on-campus events (27 October 1995, SLIS Archives). L.I.S.S. enjoyed a brief resurgence in 1997-1998, when the group created a new Web site and instituted its own listserv. But the days of lunchtime potlucks and student lockers were over, and L.I.S.S. disappeared by 2000.

The most enduring student association active during this time was a group called LISSTEN, an acronym for Library and Information Science Students to Encourage Networking. Founded by Southern California students in November 1991, LISSTEN initially sought to speak for distance education students who felt invisible to the SJSU bureaucracy. As its first undertaking, LISSTEN surveyed Fullerton-based students to discover what they wanted in a student organization. With an impressive 74% response rate, distance students asked that LISSTEN "promote better communication" with San José, work to establish ties with the local professional community, and serve as a liaison between students and faculty "to voice student concerns" (LISSTEN survey, 1992, p.1).

With the advent of email and the Web, the north and south campuses became increasingly integrated and distance-education students' communication complaints waned. LISSTEN's mission evolved accordingly, and after a few years, its focus became more programmatic and professionally oriented. In May 1993, LISSTEN sponsored its first career fair, a day-long event that continues to this day. LISSTEN began organizing the annual graduation in 1994, a responsibility it maintained for over a decade. Other annual LISSTEN events include a professional associations day (typically held in the fall of each year), a "Read-a-thon" during ALA's Banned Books Week, and a resume-writing workshop. LISSTEN also produced in 1994 a "Student Survival Handbook," which still exists on the LISSTEN Web site.

LISSTEN's most enduring project has been its monthly newsletter, the *Call Number*. In fact, the *Call Number* predates the organization by several months. The *Call Number* began as a one-page printed publication that was distributed to students in their classes. The first issue (which lacked a name at the time[33]) contained a call for students to form a new student association and other small items about professional association meetings, new registration procedures, time and place of that semester's comprehensive exams, and recent scholarship winners. Future *Call Numbers* would become increasingly substantive, and within a few years the newsletter was a multipage publication with regular columns including "People Behind the Names," "Administrative Agenda," "Connections," and "Alumni Corner." In 2006, LISSTEN became the student association for the entire campus, representing students' voices on SLIS committees and helping to organize student events. The *Call Number*, having gone online in 2002, currently serves as the student newsletter for the entire SLIS program.

In recent years, SLIS student associations have moved away from a regional orientation to focus more on professional interests and commonalities. In 1994, students organized an American Library Association chapter (ALASC) to promote and support student involvement in the ALA. This organization was named ALA's student chapter of the year in 2000 and again in 2009. In 2002, students interested in archives and records management established a student chapter of the Society of American Archivists (SAASC) to sponsor events and tours relating to that professional specialization. These groups, both of which are official affiliates of the national associations,

[33] Richard Moore can be credited with coming up with the name Call Number.

have taken pains to involve students regardless of where they reside, using SLIS technologies and social networks to cover events.

Conclusion

In the spring of 2007, San José State University's School of Library and Information Science was once again up for accreditation review by the American Library Association. As part of this process, the school administration, faculty, and staff prepared a thoroughgoing report in which the school assessed its current status and future goals. "SLIS serves over 1800 students throughout the state of California and beyond," the report opened, "preparing graduates for careers in public, school, academic, and special libraries, as well as in archives, records management, and a wide range of settings within the information industry" (p. i). SLIS took pains to demonstrate to the ALA that although its students did not necessarily attend classes on the San José State campus, they all earned the same MLIS degree. As the report explained: "With classrooms, offices, and services located in San José and in Fullerton, and through extensive and comprehensive instructional technologies, services, and support available through the Web, all students receive the same curriculum and the same Master's Degree in Library and Information Science" (p. 95). San José State was not a distance program that offered extension classes. It was one school, unified in spirit as well as substance.

San José State's success in becoming the largest MLIS program in the world was the culmination of its aggressive and independent approach to delivering professional education. Since its beginning, SLIS has sought to serve the California library community by first preparing teacher-librarians and then expanding into other professional areas as circumstances required. Throughout its history, the school has demonstrated an entrepreneurial spirit, willing to take risks and to persevere despite frustrating obstacles and disappointing setbacks. SLIS also evinced a democratic streak based on the belief that qualified individuals should have the chance to obtain a professional degree even if it meant taking the entire coursework during the summer session or online. Finally, SLIS has always been interested in cutting-edge technology. From the use of closed-circuit television in the 1950s to microfilmed course readings in the 1970s to the delivery of courses on the World Wide Web, SLIS has used technological tools to expand its program and remain relevant.

At the time of this writing SLIS has 2,868 students and 180 full- and part-time faculty worldwide. It offers nearly 100 course sections each semester, and its graduates can be found in information organizations across the country and throughout the world. Indeed, when the Carnegie Corporation and the *New York Times* announced the winners of their national "I Love My Librarian" award in December 2008, two of the ten recipients were SLIS alumni: Jean Amaral, a 2006 graduate now employed as a reference librarian at Antioch University New England in Keene, New Hampshire; and Amy Cheney, class of 2002, who works with incarcerated youth in Northern California's Alameda County Juvenile Justice Center. A third recipient of this national award was Dr. Margaret Lincoln, a valued member of SLIS's part-time faculty pool.

Conclusion

On a cool November evening in 2004, more than 130 SLIS faculty, alumni, and librarians gathered at the historic St. Claire Hotel in downtown San José to celebrate the school's fiftieth anniversary as an MLIS program. Speakers at the lavish cocktail party included SLIS Director Blanche Woolls, California Library Association President and SLIS alum Danis Kreimeier, and California State Librarian and SLIS advisory council member Susan Hildreth. The event's intent, however, was to honor the thousands of SLIS alumni who had shaped California libraries for the past 50 years.

As part of the anniversary tribute, SLIS's Alumni Association created an electronic guestbook and encouraged former students to reminisce about their time in school.[34] Many offered memories of their favorite SLIS faculty—a party at Mildred Chatton's house, dinner with Jim Healey at a local Ethiopian restaurant, chatting with Terry Crowley in his "cave-like office" filled with "piles and piles of books and papers." "I wanted to live there," admitted Pat Horn Fell (1997), "but there wasn't room." Mary Walsh, who graduated in 1976, retained an image of Shirley Hopkinson: "As students, we all loved the fact that Professor Shirley Hopkinson's mother, who was quite elderly at the time, would walk over every afternoon from their place across San Fernando [Street], to pick up Shirley after school. Her mother was a petite bird of a woman, always wearing a scarf and coat. It was such a sweet gesture on both of their parts, and we loved watching them walk out of the door together."

[34] The memory book can still be accessed at http://slisgroups.sjsu.edu/alumni/guestbook/gbs1.4/

Time spent in SLIS's classrooms also made a lasting impression on former students, particularly when the school resided on the top floor of old Wahlquist Hall.[35] Who could forget the classrooms with their "burnt orange walls" and "rag tag collection of period seating?" Then there was the "ride and pray" elevator whose regular breakdowns kept students in good physical shape. "I LOVED that the library school was at the top of this old, almost creepy, building," recalled Monica Smith, class of 2003. "You would walk into this old, empty library, take the rickety old elevator to the top floor (praying all the way), and there was the library school!" Nicole Warren (1997) described sitting in class, gazing at the mountains from the sixth-floor window, and "feeling that I was in the right place doing a good thing."

As SLIS moved to hybrid and online classes, students' memories shifted to carpools, parking lots, cheap hotels, and informal meetings at Burger King (San Jose) and El Torito Restaurant (Fullerton). "There are so many memories," Paula Paggi (2004) wrote. "Driving to Fullerton on many weekends, meeting and making friends from San Diego to Santa Barbara, having such great professors that prepared me to be successful as an LMT. When I started, I thought, 'How will I ever do it?' and I look back and wonder, 'Where did the time go?'"

Students shared memories of courses and assignments, most notably the terrors of the comprehensive exam and its successor, the Culminating Experience. Melodie Frances (1992) recalled that the Rodney King Riots erupted the night before her class took their comprehensive exam. Etched in her mind is the noise of helicopters flying overhead as she wrote her essays. Chad Stephenson (2002) relived turning in his culminating papers before the 5 p.m. deadline. He had just 5 minutes to spare because his printer had taken 45 minutes to print the required two copies of his CE papers. Darla Wegener (2000) described her own deadline horrors: "computer and printer problems, keys and culminating papers locked in car, CLA presentations, and rain all in the twenty-four hours before my culminating papers were due."

[35] Built in 1942, Wahlquist North housed the university library until the bulk of the library collection was moved to Clark Hall in 1982. Wahlquist was demolished in 2006 to make way for the new Dr. Martin Luther King, Jr. Library on the same site.

SLIS students were on the front lines of the computer revolution, and many described their memorable experiences working with new technologies. Taking classes in the early 1970s, John Kenny (1973) remembered struggling with a typewriter to create perfect catalog cards. "There were no integrated library systems then," he wrote. "We used punched cards." Just a few years later, Joseph Augustino (1976) was learning COBOL programming as part of his coursework, while in the 1980s, Ruth Phebus (1987) was introduced to a new system called Dialog, carefully timing her searches stay to within the allotted (and costly) online minutes. Christine Holmes (1995) remembered collaborating with another student to load Mosaic (the first Web browser) onto the school's computers, while Pat Horn Fell (1997) described the "ozone smell of the computer lab, and the incredibly irritating clicking squeals of the dot-matrix printers." Dave Shannon (1993) also commented on "all the interest in this new technology" and how "desperate" students were to figure it out:

> One of the few books available at the time was "Zen and the Art of the Internet: A Beginner's Guide" by Brendan Kehoe. I purchased it, still couldn't figure out how to get an ftp file with a .TAR extension so I emailed Brendan Kehoe to ask him how it should be done. I'm still waiting for his response . . . ."

For many students, it was the camaraderie with other students that made their time at SJSU so special. As James Scott (1999) expressed it,

> Hands down, the best thing about SLIS was the bevy of great people that I was able to meet. Like a lot of folks, I moved to California from somewhere else (Portland), looking for something better. Little did I know that I'd hit the mother lode; surely, the relationships developed and connections made through SJSU will stay with me for years to come. Coming to SJSU and SLIS was one of the best decisions I've ever made.

Indeed, many SLIS alumni expressed gratitude for the education they received and the impact that an MLIS degree had on their lives. The earliest entry came from Valerie Hicks, a 1963 graduate who wrote: "I have such fond memories of San Jose State's Library School and the great instructors who taught me. I have served in various librarian capacities first in Lompoc then for over 30 years at Chabot College in Hayward. I've loved every minute, (well, ok, almost every minute) and found that the education I obtained from our library school to have prepared me beautifully for my life's work." Fred Gertler, class of 1977, shares these strong feelings about his library science education: "Library school at SJSU SLIS changed my life. Thanks to my classmates and the faculty, I found direction, purpose, and passion, and I will always be grateful for that."

Fred's feelings are particularly poignant given the fact he earned his degree during the lean years when the school's very survival was in question. Penny Peck (1977) was a classmate of Fred's and described the climate of that time:

> I graduated in December 1977, part of a group of 90 who were motivated to graduate quickly because the library school was losing its accreditation (just temporarily; it was re-accredited 5 years later). Ironically, Proposition 13 passed the month before, so we newly-minted MLIS went out into a bleak job market that didn't really have much for us—in my case, it took 9 years to get a full-time librarian job. But the life experience I gained was also very important.

Gerry Rowland (1979) began his MLIS program just after the ALA had denied SLIS's reaccreditation bid in 1976. "Those were tense times," Gerry recalled, and as a TA he spent "considerable time with the COA reps" and "celebrated with all when accreditation was restored." Then came Proposition 13 and Gerry ended up moving to Iowa to find his first professional position.

Yet despite the downturn in the late seventies and eighties, students like Fred, Penny, and Gerry persevered and carved out meaningful and productive careers. Fred, who served for many years as president of

SLIS's alumni association, landed a job with an early database company and then went on to a 30-year career as an academic librarian, retiring in summer 2008 as associate dean of the University of Pacific's Library. Penny eventually found a job as a children's services librarian at the San Leandro Public Library, and in 2006 published a textbook, *Crash Course in Children's Services*, with Libraries Unlimited. She has also taught children's services courses for SLIS since 1994. Gerry spent his 27-year career in Iowa, working first as a public library director then as a librarian and library consultant at the Iowa State Library. He became well known for his environmental activism and his role in protecting Iowa's river system. These three alumni, along with thousands of other graduates, represent the best of SLIS in their accomplishments and repute, their contributions to libraries and their local communities, and their efforts to guide the next generation of information professionals.

San José State University's School of Library and Information Science also confronted initial discouragement and adversity yet persevered to become the world's largest MLIS program. Starting on the eve of the Great Depression, SLIS originally sought to educate teachers to manage their school libraries and to develop in children a love of reading and learning. SLIS continued to specialize in teacher-librarianship until after the Second World War and played a key part in incorporating new postwar technologies into school libraries. As San José State evolved from a teacher's college to a comprehensive undergraduate and graduate university, SLIS was able to expand and diversify, adding new faculty and specializations in the 1950s and 1960s. SLIS weathered the hardships and uncertainties of the 1970s, which included an administrative and financial crisis on campus and the loss of accreditation by the ALA, and then rebounded in the 1980s to claim a larger and larger role in educating California's information professionals. Being located in the Silicon Valley certainly aided SLIS's reputation and growth. The program capitalized on the region's technology resources and talent to add cutting-edge information systems to its curriculum and course delivery, as well as to find employment for many of its promising graduates. SLIS's willingness to experiment with flexible scheduling was also an important factor in recruiting individuals to a program that had traditionally attracted older, re-entry students. The turning point, however, came in 1989, when SLIS officially committed itself to developing a statewide library school and established its first official branch at California State University, Fullerton. A pioneer in distance learning, SLIS was among the first programs to experiment with innovative learning technologies and new modes of course delivery almost as soon as they became available. As a result, SLIS has been able to build a stable and comprehensive library and information science program that is now global in scope and influence.

Appendix 1

SJSU School of Library and Information Science Chronology

1857 Minns School founded in San Francisco

1862 California State Legislature passes legislation transforming the Minns School into the California State Normal School

1871 California State Normal School relocates to San José

1887 California State Normal School renamed San José State Normal School

1921 California Department of Education established and San José State Normal School becomes San José State Teachers College under its jurisdiction

1924 American Library Association's (ALA) Board of Education for Librarianship established

1925 ALA adopts first accreditation standards for library science programs

1928 California State Board of Education enacts its first education code and establishes the "Special Credential in Librarianship;" the Board also approves state teachers colleges offering nonteaching bachelor's degrees; the Department of Librarianship is created, with Joyce Backus serving as department chair; first library science classes taught in fall 1928

1929 State Department of Education authorizes San José State to offer a BA with a major in librarianship; first summer school courses taught in library science; a library certificate program also established in the Junior College

1930 Dora Smith, first full-time faculty member, hired; Bibliophiles student organization established

1935 San José State Teachers College becomes San José State College

1939 Department of Librarianship discontinues its Junior College certificate program

1946 State Board of Education authorizes San José State College to award master's degrees

1949 Department of Librarianship establishes specialization in Library Work with Children in Public Libraries

1950 Dora Smith named department head

1951 New ALA accreditation standards recognize master's level degree only; Department of Librarianship and Department of Education form the Division of Education

1952 Alpha Beta Alpha library science fraternity established

1953 Department of Librarianship begins extended day program by offering evening classes

1954 San José State approves graduate degree program in school librarianship; second master's program in Curriculum Materials also created in partnership with the Audio Visual Department

1957 First off-site course taught in Santa Cruz

1958 Library Science Department uses closed-circuit television in its classes

1959 Leslie H. Janke appointed department chair

1960 Specialization in Public Library Service added to library science curriculum

1961 San José State joins the newly founded California State University System

1963 Fisher Act, passed in 1961 making the California Teaching Credential a postgraduate degree, goes into effect

1964 Bachelor's degree in librarianship eliminated

1967 Specialization in College and Special Libraries added to library science curriculum

1968 Department of Librarianship separates from the School of Education and becomes an independent department under the Graduate Studies Division

1969 Department of Librarianship accredited by the ALA; LIBR 283, Documentation and Information Retrieval, added to the curriculum

1970 Concerned Library Students (CLS), a student advocacy group, formed

1971 Omega chapter of Beta Phi Mu and Alumni Association organized

1972 San José State College renamed California State University, San José

1974 CSU, San José officially changed to San José State University; joint program in School Media established with Department of Instructional Technology; interdisciplinary MS degree in Computer and Information Science also created

1975 ALA Committee on Accreditation votes not to reaccredit SJSU's MLS program

1977 CSU approves changing the Master of Arts in Librarianship degree to Master of Library Science; Department of Librarianship becomes the Division of Library Science

1979 San José State's MLS degree reaccredited by the ALA

1981 Guy Marco appointed director

1983 Robert Wagers becomes interim director

1985 Division of Library Science renamed Division of Library and Information Science; James Healey selected as new director; degree name changed from Master of Library Science to Master of Library and Information Science

1988 Library and Information Science Students (LISS) created

1989 SJSU opens branch campus at California State University, Fullerton, and begins teaching library science classes there in the fall

1991 LISSTEN (Library and Information Science Students to Encourage Networking) formed

1992 Division of Library and Information Science renamed School of Library and Information Science (SLIS)

1993 Stuart Sutton becomes SLIS director

1994 ALA Student Chapter (ALASC) established

1995 First interactive video courses taught between San José State and CSU Fullerton

1996 Bill Fisher serves as interim director

1997 Blanche Woolls appointed SLIS director; archival studies specialization added

2000 ALASC named ALA Student Chapter of the Year

2001 First completely online classes taught

2002 Society of American Archivists Student Chapter (SAASC) authorized

2005 Ken Haycock assumes SLIS directorship; Executive MLIS program inaugurated

2007 SLIS opens virtual campus in Second Life; Association for Library and Information Science Education (ALISE) gives SLIS its 2007 Pratt-Severn Faculty Innovation Award; *US News and World Report* ranks SLIS #1 in LIS e-learning, #6 in teacher-librarianship, and #30 in its MLIS program

2008 Master of Archives and Records Administration (MARA) established; SLIS launches a gateway PhD program with Australia's Queensland University of Technology

2009 *US News and World Report* ranks SLIS's MLIS program at #22 and its school-librarianship program at #4; ALA names ALASC Student Chapter of the Year; SLIS program goes completely online, officially becoming the "Global e-Campus in Library and Information Science"

Appendix 2

School of Library and Information Science Directors and Faculty

SLIS Directors (Years as Administrator)

Backus, Joyce (1928-1950)
Smith, Dora (1950-1959)
Janke, Leslie (1959-1981)
Marco, Guy (1981-1983)
Wagers, Robert (Interim, 1983-1985)
Healey, James (1985-1993)
Sutton, Stuart (1993-1996)
Fisher, Bill (Interim, 1996-1997)
Woolls, Blanche (1997-2005)
Haycock, Ken (2005- present)

SLIS Faculty (Years with SLIS)

Note: Until the 1960s, SLIS had few regular full-time instructors and considered part-time faculty and college librarians as regular faculty. Faculty in other departments, such as James Dolby (Mathematics) and James Cabeceiras (Instructional Technology), also taught classes for SLIS. This list includes individuals who were not officially full-time department members, but who contributed to SLIS's development, nonetheless.

Backus, Joyce (1923-1950)
Bailey, Lucy (1936-1938)
Baillie, Stuart (1965-1978)
Baldwin, Ruth Marie (1946-1949)
Banathy, Bela (1968-1971)
Beattie, Emelyn (1926-1930)
Bernier, Anthony (2005-present)
Bodart, Joni Richards (2006-present)
Bullock, Helen (1929-1962)
Burns, Nancy (1991-2006)
Cabeceiras, James (1971-c.1981)
Ceppos, Karen (1982-1997)
Chatton, Mildred Vick (1968-1980)
Clark, Kristen (2007-present)
Costantino, Connie (2005-2008)
Crowley, Terence (1978-2000)
Dikeman, Robert (1979-c.1984)
Dolby, James L. (1966-1985)
Dowlin, Kenneth (1997-2006)
Faires, Debbie (2001-present)
Fisher, Bill (1988-present)
Fisher, Jane (2006-present)
Ford, Charlotte (2005-2008)
Franks, Patricia (2008-present)
Fuller, Daniel (2002-present)
Gitler, Robert (1931-1942)
Groves, Elizabeth (1942-1945)
Hafter, Ruth (1986-2000)
Hansen, Debra (1989-present)
Haycock, Ken (2005-present)
Healey, James (1985-1995)
Hicks, Warren (1968-c.1979)
Hopkinson, Shirley (1959-1992)
Jackson, Joy Belle (1926-c. 1931)
Janke, Leslie (1956-1981)
Johnson, Clifford Robert (1978-1989)
Jones, Stephanie (1990-1994)

Karpuk, Deborah (2002-2007)
Kelley, Arthur (1928-1943)
Kemp, Jeremy (2001-present)
Kerr, Ruby (1928-1929)
Lauritzen, Robert (1952-1986)
Lieberman, Janice (1967-c.1984)
Limbocker, Marjorie (1945-1966)
Lindberg, Lori (2002-present)
Liu, Geoffrey (1995-present)
Liu, Ziming (2000-present)
Loertscher, David (1996-present)
Loventhal, Milton (1959-1992)
Luo, Lili (2007-present)
Main, Linda (1985-present)
Marco, Guy (1981-1983)
Martin, Laura K. (1938-1939)
Matthews, Joe (2006-2009)
Mishoff, Willard Oral (1962-1966)
Molto, Mavis (1991-1993)
Munday, Jerome (1955-1988)
Norell, Irene (1959-1985)
Nunes, Gertrude Memmler (1944-1945)
Olsen, Harold (1977-c.1984)
Pai, Edward (1992-2006)
Pastine, Maureen (1980-1985)
Pulling, Hazel (1938-1940)
Purser, Frances Hichborn (1931-1936)
Rosen, Elizabeth McClure (1985-c.1990)
Schmidt, C. James (1992-2009)
Smith, Dora V. (1930-1959)
Smith, Elisabeth (1961-1962)
Speer, Eunice (1940-1945)
Stone, Clarence Walter (1970-c.1972)
Sutton, Stuart (1993-1996)
Tessier, Judith (1987-2006)
Tyson, Edwin (1966-c.1974)
Vander Ploeg, Jeannette (1930-1956)

Wagers, Robert (1976-2006)
Weedman, Judith (1995-present)
West, Martha (1969-1978)
Wichers, Jean Elaine (1965-1983)
Wittig, Donald (1968-1970)
Wood, William Bliss (1967-1978)
Woolls, Blanche (1997-present)

References

American Library Association Archives. (1922-1954). Library education program files. University of Illinois, Archives. Urbana, IL.

Backus, J. (1929). The college library. In E. Greathead (Ed.), *The story of an inspiring past: Historical sketch of the San Jose State Teachers College from 1862-1928* (pp. 44-45). San Jose: San Jose State Teachers College.

Backus, J. (1938, February). Training for elementary school library service. *Western Journal of Education,* 10-11.

Beymer, M. (1933, October). What's in a name? Editorial comments. *Bulletin of the School Library Association of California, 6*(1), 9.

Buckland, M. (Ed.) (1999). *Robert Gitler and the Japan Library School: An autobiographical Narrative.* Lanham, MD: Scarecrow Press.

Bulletin of the San Jose State Teachers College. (1919/1921-1949/1950). San José: San José State University.

California Library Association. (1929). *Handbook and proceedings of the annual meeting.* Los Angeles: California Library Association.

Carroll, C. E. (1970). *The professionalization of education for librarianship.* Metuchen, NJ: Scarecrow Press.

Chapman, P. D. (1981). Schools as sorters: Testing and tracking in California, 1910-1925. *Journal of Social History, 14*(4), 701-717.

Coulter, E. (1932). Library schools committee [report] (pp. 62-63). *California Library Association handbook and proceedings of the annual meeting*. Sacramento: California Library Association.

Crosby, O. (2000). Librarians: Information experts in the information age. *Occupational Outlook Quarterly, 44*(4), 2-15.

Crowley, T. (1998). In the beginning was the word: Lessons from students. *Journal of Education for Librarianship, 39*(3), 204-207.

Division of Library and Information Science. (1991-1992). *Bulletin*. San Jose: DLIS.

Dowlin, K. (1984). *The electronic library: The promise and the process*. New York: Neal-Schuman.

Francois, V. (1999, September 28). Demand for librarians hits an all-time high. *National Business Employment Weekly*. Retrieved from http://online.wsj.com/career/resources/documents/19990928-francois.htm.

Fullwood, M. T. (1929). Survey of California junior high school libraries. *School Library Yearbook, 3* (pp. 65-73). Chicago: American Library Association.

Gest, E. (1995, August 20). Beyond 2000: The jobs of the past, the jobs of the future. *Los Angeles Times*, pp. 26-27.

Gilbert, B. F. (1957). *Pioneers for one hundred years: San Jose State College, 1857-1957*. San Jose: San Jose State College.

Gilbert, B. F. & Burdick, C. (1980). *Washington Square, 1857-1979: The history of San Jose State University*. San Jose: San Jose State University.

Girdner, M. V. (1929). School library visions. In *Handbook and proceedings of the California Library Association* (pp. 85-88). Los Angeles: California Library Association.

Girdner, M. V. (1930). The public library versus the school library: Cooperation or duplication? (pp. 111-117). In *California Library Association handbook and proceedings of the annual meeting*. Los Angeles: California Library Association.

Gitler, R. (1941, July 1). It's not ants in the pants – but animals in the stacks. [Interview with Robert Gitler]. *Spartan Daily*. N.p.

Gitler, R. (1990). Special Joyce Backus memorial issue. *Stacks 'N' Facts: SJSU Library Newsletter, 3* (2/3), 2.

Hall, A. E. (1974). *Public elementary and secondary school library development in California, 1850-1966* (Unpublished doctoral dissertation). Columbia University, New York, NY.

Hawaiian Mission Children's Society. (1920). Sixty-eighth annual report of the Hawaiian Mission Children's Society. Honolulu: Paradise of the Pacific Print.

Haycock, K. (2008). High tech, high touch, high quality: Building the world's largest MLIS program at San José. In D. Bogart (Ed.), *The Bowker annual: Library and book trade almanac*. New York: R. R. Bowker.

Healey, J. S. (1980, Fall). Accreditation from the other side: A study of the accreditation process and its effects on three schools. *Journal of Education for Librarianship, 21*, 146-155.

Healey, J. S. (1988). The electronic library school: An alternative approach in library education. *Technical Services Quarterly, 6*(2), 17-26.

Healey, J. S. (1988). Open letter to the California library community. *CLA Newsletter, 30*(10), 9.

Healey, J. S. (1991). Distance library education. *Library Trends, 39*(4), 424-440.

Healey, J. S. (1991). Library education in California: Focus on San Jose State. *California Libraries, 1*(6), 1.

Janke, L. H. (1959, March). San Jose trains librarians via closed-circuit TV. *Bulletin of the School Library Association of California, 30*, 6.

La Torre. (1928-1960). San José: Associated Students of San José State College.

Lake, D. (1929). Survey of California senior high school libraries. *School Library Yearbook, 3* (pp. 73-76). Chicago: American Library Association.

Landfear, B. (1940, November). Visual aids: Challenge to school librarians. *Bulletin of the School Library Association of California, 12*, 12-13.

Leigh, R. D. (1952). *The California librarian education survey; A report to President Robert G. Sproul of the University of California.* New York: Columbia University.

Librarians need not take graduate work. (1941, May 26). *Spartan Daily,* N.p.

LISSTEN survey results. (1992). *The Call Number, 4*(4), 1.

Local college lauded as pioneer in librarianship. (1930, February 5). *San Jose Herald Mercury.* N.p.

Mahar, K. W. (2006). *Women filmmakers in early Hollywood.* Baltimore: Johns Hopkins University Press.

Mediavilla, C. (2008). Proposition 13: A year of chaos, panic, and disarray. *Clarion, 4*(1), 6-7.

Muhlberger, P. (2005). The Virtual Agora Project: A research design for studying democratic deliberation. *Journal of Public Deliberation, 1*(1). Retrieved from http://services.bepress.com/jpd/vol1/iss1/art5.

Parker, M. R. (1974). *A history of the Department of Librarianship at San Jose State University, 1928-1969* (Unpublished master's thesis). San José State University, San José, CA.

Potter, G. (1942, October). Reading, writing, and speaking . . . their contribution to social competence. *Childhood Education, 19,* 69-73.

Proposal for a graduate school of library and information science, University of California, Riverside. (1991, November 25). A Report Prepared by the Graduate School of Library and Information Science Task Force. (Typescript). SLIS Archives, San José State University, San José.

Rosen, E. M. (1987, winter). Educators and practitioners: A cooperative pattern of curriculum review. *Top of the News, 43*, 185-188.

San Jose program is 'the finest.' (1977, January). *American Libraries, 8*, 14.

San José State University Archives. (1920-1970). San José State University, San José, CA.

San José State University School of Library and Information Science. (2007). *2005-2007 Years in Review.* San Jose: SLIS.

San José State University School of Library and Information Science. (2007). 40 for 40 alumni celebration. San Jose: SLIS.

San José State University School of Library and Information Science. Archives. (1928-2008). San José State University, San José, CA.

Smith, D. (1938, December). Reading—a moot question. *Bulletin of the American Library Association, 32,* 1031-1040.

Smith, D. (1955, April). School library training looks ahead: A new program at San Jose State College. *California Librarian, 16,* 185, 200.

Smith, G. W. (1991, November). Library education in California: Issues and opportunities. A report of the Council of Library Directors. Long Beach, CA: California State University Office of the Chancellor. ERIC doc. 351014.

Statement concerning the accreditation appeal of San Jose State University. (1976, December). *American Libraries, 7,* 696-697.

Summer session at San Jose State. (1936, March). *California Library Association Bulletin, 7*(5), 14.

Sutton, S. A. (1993, August 27). A plan for statewide technology-mediated distance education. Typescript. SLIS Archives, San José State University, San José.

Sutton, S. A. (1996). Planning for the twenty-first century: The California State University. *Journal of the American Society for Information Science, 47*(11), 821-825.

Sutton, S., Van House, N. & Bates, M. (1995). Dimensions of practice. [Report for the] CLA Task Force on the Future of the Library Profession. Typescript. SLIS Archives.

Walsh, J. P. (2003). *San Jose State University: An interpretive history, 1950-2000.* San Jose: San Jose State University.

Walsh, J. P. (2006). *One and the same: The history of continuing education at San José State University, 1857-2007.* San José: San José State University.

Weiler, K. (1994). Women and rural school reform: California, 1900-1940. *History of Education Quarterly, 34*(1), 25-47.

Where the kitchens have no sinks. (1938, December 7). *San Jose Herald Mercury.* N.p.

White, C. M. (1976). *A historical introduction to library education: Problems and progress to 1951.* Metuchen, N.J.: Scarecrow Press.

Wichers, J. (1966, May). An approach to communimedia. *California School Libraries, 37*(4), 22-24.

Index